LIFE-DEFINING MOMENTS FROM
BOLD THOUGHT LEADERS

To RACHEL

From DAD

I wish for you a life of wealth, health, and happiness; a life in which you give to yourself the gift of patience, the virtue of reason, the value of knowledge, and the influence of faith in your own ability to dream about and to achieve worthy rewards.

– Jim Rohn

To my wonderful daughter
You are on such a great path
Looking forward to sharing
many life moments in the years
to come
So grateful for the blessing
you are in my life
Love Dad

Published by
Lessons From Network
www.LessonsFromNetwork.com

Distributed by
Lessons From Network
P.O. Box 93927
Southlake, TX 76092
817-379-2300
www.LessonsFromNetwork.com/books

ISBN: 978-0-9983125-4-5 (Paperback)

Printed in the United States of America.

LIFE-DEFINING MOMENTS FROM
BOLD THOUGHT LEADERS

**Receive Your Special Bonuses for
Buying the *Life-Defining Moments* Book**

To Receive Your Special Bonuses
Send an Email to info@LessonsFromDefiningMoments.com
with *Gifts* in the subject

DISCLAIMER

The information in this book is not meant to replace the advice of a certified professional. Please consult a licensed advisor in matters relating to your livelihood including your mental and physical health, finances, business, family planning, education, and spiritual practices.

If you choose to attempt any of the methods mentioned in this book, the authors and publisher advise you to take full responsibility for your safety and know your limits. The authors and publisher are not liable for any damages or negative consequences from any treatment, action, application, or preparation to any person reading or following the information in this book.

Neither the publisher nor the individual authors shall be liable for any physical, psychological, emotional, financial, or commercial damages, including, but not limited to, special, incidental, consequential, or other damages to the readers of this book.

The content of each chapter is the sole expression and opinion of its author and not necessarily that of the publisher. No warranties or guarantees are expressed or implied by the publisher's choice to include any of the content in this volume.

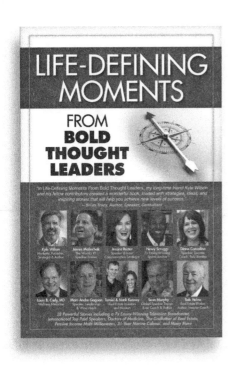

To order additional copies, including quantity discounts, of *Life-Defining Moments from Bold Thought Leaders* see below.

Dedication

To Mom, Dad, Jim Rohn and other angels looking down who inspire and light my path.

Acknowledgement

To Takara Sights for your endless hours of work and passion in this book as our editor and project manager! This makes book number four for you and me! A thousand praises! You are a rockstar! #millennialsrule

Foreword

by Kyle Wilson

'm such a believer in the power of stories to transform lives. My mentor, friend, and 18-year business partner, Jim Rohn often talked about the faith transference that happens when we share our own successes and wins with others.

When I'm in a coaching or consulting session or I'm sharing from stage, so much of what I share are stories and examples from my own experiences as well as other people's because numbers and facts often time get lost, but stories can transform.

Sometimes the story you hear or read is not for you, but for a friend or a family member.

Over the years I've published and sold millions of books with titles from Jim Rohn, Denis Waitley, Mark Victor Hansen, Zig Ziglar, Brian Tracy, and more. This past year I've published three titles, *Passionistas*, *The Little Black Book of Fitness*, and *Mom & Dadpreneurs*. The common thread in all these books is, they are made up of authentic stories with the goal to help you find inspiration, validation, and new breakthroughs.

And this book, *Life-Defining Moments From Bold Thoughts Leaders*, is especially near and dear to my heart.

You see, as we were closing in on the end of 2016, I knew I wanted to take the next step with my Kyle Wilson Inner Circle Mastermind group. How could I spend more focused time with a more intimate group of people?

From that decision this book was birthed. In 2017 many members from my Inner Circle came together for a more intimate experience of mentoring, growing, and taking our businesses and lives to the next level. And this is not just any group. This group included a 7x Emmy-winner, a Colonel in the Marines, two doctors, a world renowned speaking coach, real estate investors, entrepreneurs, speakers, business and life coaches, authors, and more.

Over a year we bonded and became very vulnerable, intimate, and close. From that place many of these stories were unearthed.

This book has stories of overcoming financial ruin and battling health challenges, both mental and physical. There are stories of how some handled and survived personal and family tragedies and abuse. It has stories of persistence and courage. It has stories of redemption and stories of unconventional approaches to life's challenges.

Our ultimate hope is that these stories will help you create positive, ever-lasting change in your life and move you into action!

I'm honored by this group's courage and commitment to make a difference in the world. These leaders have decided to truly get out of the safe and comfortable to share their life-defining moments with you.

Enjoy!

With much love and gratitude!

Kyle Wilson
Founder LessonsFromNetwork.com, Jim Rohn International (JimRohn.com), YourSuccessStore.com and KyleWilson.com

TABLE OF CONTENTS

I found every single successful person I've ever spoken to had a turning point. The turning point was when they made a clear, specific unequivocal decision that they were not going to live like this anymore; they were going to achieve success. Some people make that decision at 15 and some people make it at 50, and most people never make it at all.

– Brian Tracy

CHAPTER 1

The Jim Rohn Story
As Though Everything is a Miracle
by Kyle Wilson

'll never forget being on a radio interview and the host asking, "To have been Jim Rohn's 18 year business partner and to have worked with so many legends you must have been an outstanding young adult...class president, business degree, etc. Can you tell us your story?"

Well, I was far from being class president and from having any business degrees. Although I was a bit of an entrepreneur in high school, it had more to do with selling drugs. Attending class was not my strong suit. In fact, I still have an occasional dream (nightmare) where I don't end up graduating at all.

I did have a great upbringing. I grew up in Vernon, Texas, a small town of 12,000 people. I was the youngest of four. My parents were honest, kind, supportive, and loving. But they were also taxed with their time and resources with four kids and with my two oldest siblings in out-of-state college. That created more independence for me.

Although I had always been a hard worker, having a job since age 15, at age 19 I had a significant emotional experience and made some major changes. I gave up drugs, alcohol, and partying. I was ready to get serious. I started my first real business, a car detailing shop. That lead to having a service station, which within a few years became one of the more successful service stations in town: open 24/7, 10 employees, on the highway, with school bus contracts and selling just about every kind of service. It was a lot of hard work and I learned lot of valuable lessons. Hard lessons. Painful lessons. But it was an invaluable experience.

After a few years, at age 26, I decided I needed a change. I would sell my business and make the big move to Dallas, three hours away.

Through several serendipitous events, I received an opportunity to work for a company as a sales rep, then later started a different business, which led me to attend a sales seminar. There I met the promoter of the seminar, Jerry Haines, who hired me to become a rep for him.

Working for Jerry meant learning to cold call companies, going in and giving a 30 minute presentation, and then selling tickets to an upcoming seminar. Cold calling was new for me, but the even bigger challenge was presenting in front of people and THEN having to sell them tickets to an event.

This was WAY out of my comfort zone!

But, I felt in a bubble. I felt I had to give it a try. If I could do this, it would give me so much personal power. So I went for it.

After a few months I became Jerry's top guy in Dallas. Not because I was so good, but because the other 10 people he brought on all quit. It was a tough, tough business and candidly, the financial model was broken. But I was an optimist, and I wanted to make it work.

I was putting on five or six seminars a year while working for Jerry. Then in 1990, Jerry called me one day and said we were changing who we would be promoting, and the new guy was his mentor, Jim Rohn.

I quickly became an avid student of Jim's teaching. I was frequently replaying a 60 minute cassette Jerry gave me. I would get to have dinner with Jim every two months the night before our event and, of course, I took copious notes during each seminar.

As much as I loved promoting Jim, I knew the financial model of the company I was with was broken, and that I had to leave Jerry and go out on my own if I was ever going to be able to make a living and if I wanted to go from 200-300 people to 2000+ people in a room.

Although I was recognized as the top performer in Jerry's company, I had become deeply in debt. So I made the tough decision and left the company.

For my first solo event I knew I needed to go to a new place. So, my wife and I made the leap and moved from Dallas to Atlanta. We got a U-Haul and used our Chevron credit card to not just buy gas to get there but to also buy food. Yes, we lived on food from those Chevron stations with a mini grocery store for days; we had no other option.

Before we left Dallas I researched potential hotel venues to hold the first event. When we pulled into town we went straight to the top candidate: The Westin in downtown Atlanta. We loved the hotel. They were excited to host us and they did not ask for an immediate deposit.

I told them we needed to find a place to stay, and I asked if I could trade them five tickets to the future event to be held there in exchange for our stay at the hotel for five nights. They said YES. That was like a miracle to me.

That first day I was hammering the phones to find a corporate apartment for us to live for three months as well as trying to book meetings for me to go speak at and start selling tickets. A few hours into making calls, the hotel called me and said they needed my credit card to pay for all the phone calls I was making (I had already racked up over $100 of calls). I asked if there was any way I could trade another ticket for unlimited use of their phone. They said YES! Wow, another mini miracle!

I found the perfect corporate apartment. And they agreed to do a 50/50 cash and trade. It was the nicest place we ever stayed and the only trade I ever pulled off with an apartment in all my years as a promoter. Now the big ask. Would they accept the 50% cash in 30 days versus me paying them upfront. They said YES.

Also I was able to book my first talk for the very next day, 11 weeks before the event. I went in and spoke to eight people. Seven ended up buying. I had no fliers, no tickets, and no credit card merchant account (I was in the works of getting that setup), just a date, location, and the promise that I was telling the truth. I asked if they would pay me in cash or write a check to me personally. And they all said YES.

For me, these were each miracles in support of this bold step of faith to go on my own.

We were off and running.

It had taken four years of me being a promoter to go from modest numbers of a few hundred people to now starting to get 2,000-3,000 people consistently. And one of the major shifts came when I talked my wife, Heidi, into joining me. She had never been in sales, had never used the phone to book appointments, and for sure had never given presentations to companies and then sold them at the end on going to a seminar. "That's a crazy idea," my friend Gordon told me when I suggested the missing piece to my seminar business was to recruit my wife to leave her secretarial job and join me. But that is exactly what I did, and she came on board, learned the process, and was a superstar.

That first event in Atlanta was Brian Tracy and Og Mandino and we got 1300 people. Then Chicago was 1800, next Washington DC was 2100, and then Sacramento was 2600. After that first event in Atlanta I was able to go back to Jerry and hire Jim Rohn to be part of my events starting in Chicago.

We had mastered the formula. We would go into a new city four times a year promoting an event with two speakers using Brian Tracy, Og Mandino, or Jim Rohn. That gave us plenty of time to get moved in, set up, book our calendar full of speaking engagements, fill a huge room for an event, and then afterwards have two weeks to celebrate and be on to the next city.

We left Sacramento March of 1993, after one of our all-time best events with Brian Tracy and Jim Rohn, and headed to our next city, Kansas City.

Surprising life events made the Kansas City event very difficult.

During the promotion time of the event, my dad passed away after fighting cancer and Heidi got pregnant and was sick pretty much the whole time we were there. Both impacted my ability to put on a world-class event.

The day finally came. The event was great but not nearly as successful as the previous events.

At the end of the event, I met with Jim Rohn. He and Jerry had split up. There had been a huge financial loss involved. Jerry had been my mentor and had impacted my life. But after Jim made it clear he and Jerry would not be partners anymore, that night I made Jim an offer for me to launch Jim Rohn International.

After Kansas City, Heidi and I knew she could not continue her role while pregnant. I also now had an opportunity to partner full-time with the best speaker in the world (that's how I saw Jim). So I now shifted my focus to full-time launching JRI.

Jim was the speaker, the world class philosopher. I was the marketer. At the time Jim had no customer list and only a handful of products.

Within the first 12 months, I took Jim from 20 dates at $4,000 each to over 110 dates at $10,000 each (and eventually $25,000 per talk).

I went to work on a product line including creating and launching a viral quote booklet that went on to sell over six million copies.

My focus was to build a customer list and a product line using what I call The Wheel.

Within two years, business was booming and we had a team of almost 20 people.

While building JRI I found that Jim was the gateway to personal development for so many people. With my focus on list and customer building, I decided to launch YourSuccessStore.com where I could market other speakers' products and also book them into the companies I was booking Jim into. YourSuccessStore included good friends Brian Tracy, Les Brown, Mark Victor Hansen, Zig Ziglar, Jeffrey Gitomer, and many more.

In 1999, with the internet taking off, I started creating multiple publications including *Messages From The Masters*, *Quotes From The Masters*, *Jim Rohn Ezine*, *The Slight Edge Newsletter*, and many more.

That all led to over one million subscribers and over 100 intellectual products (books, CDs, DVDs, and packages) plus putting on some pretty special two and three day events.

In 2007, my team and I decided to sell Jim Rohn International, Your Success Store, and some other properties to Video Plus, who was also buying *Success* Magazine.

After selling to *Success* in late 2007, I stayed on for a year helping with the transition

Shortly after the sale, Jim Rohn was diagnosed with an incurable condition, pulmonary fibrosis. He was 78 at the time. It was so hard for Jim and for all of us watching on. Jim truly believed he would live to be 100.

One day Reed Bilbray and I talked about what if we could do a special tribute video for Jim. If I could get the people together, produce, and edit it, then *Success* would supply the team and resources.

We were able to get so many of Jim's contemporaries like Zig Ziglar, John Maxwell, Brian Tracy, and Denis Waitley, along with many good friends and former team members to fly into Dallas or Los Angeles, and we were able to get their stories about Jim's impact on their lives.

A few months before Jim passed, I had the greatest honor of my life to fly into Los Angeles and visit Jim where he was staying and watch with him the edited video that featured classic Jim Rohn stories and topics mixed in with over 50 different people sharing their love and appreciation for Jim. Jim was blown away. I'm forever thankful for Reed and Stewart Johnson wanting to make this happen and letting me run lead on it.

I will be forever grateful and honored for the 18 life-changing years I was friends, biz partners and mentored by Jim Rohn! I owe Jim everything!

After Jim's passing, I stayed retired for almost seven years, spending time with my two kids during their early teen years.

Now I'm back building businesses again, hosting my Inner Circle Masterminds in Dallas and LA, hosting my Mentoring Group (which includes all the contributors in this book), launching multiple #1 best-selling books, and doing coaching and consulting for speakers, authors, investors, entrepreneurs, and companies.

My story is NOT a cookie cutter story.

The late great William Bailey, one of Jim Rohn's main mentors, once shared with me, "Kyle there is no way you could have ever predicted meeting Jim Rohn. You didn't even know who he was. But you keep doing your best, finding mentors, being hungry, and your true, unique gift made room for itself."

I tell people all the time that we learn best by doing! I couldn't have predicted getting in the seminar business, I had to learn that from the ground up. Then I became an agent, first with Jim but then also people like Denis Waitley, Ron White, Chris Widener, and more. I had to learn that. Then I learned how to create products and training programs. Then I learned to self publish books. I sold over 6 million books, but I never took a class. I learned it by doing it.

Then came the internet. I didn't follow the popular plan every one else was doing. I believe marketing is connecting the dots. And with the internet, I just started connecting the marketing dots (I was not a tech guy and didn't even know how to type, but I understood marketing and how to connect the dots). Then came building a team of 20 employees. Running a team was one of the hardest things I had to learn (and painful). But we built an amazing team that included profit sharing and celebrations. Then I had to learn to sell a business.

The past few years it's been all about reinventing myself, as I have always tried to do the past 25 years. The tactics change, the environment changes, the people often change, but the principles don't change.

People always comment about how amazing the people are that attend my events and Inner Circle meetings, and I say it's because I attract Jim Rohn fans and Jim Rohn people are principled based.

My life has been a series of what would seem like serendipitous meetings and changes and shifts.

Albert Einstein said, "There are two ways to live your life. One is as though nothing is a miracle. The other is as though everything is a miracle." I'm beyond blessed and honored to have worked with and been mentored by so many amazing people.

Last thoughts.

Always look for how to be valuable. Don't be a great networker, be a great value bringer.

Fish. Don't hunt. Fishing is creating value and then finding ways to attract the people you want to work with. As a promoter and marketer I've attracted amazing people by creating things people want to be a part of.

Work with good people. Zig Ziglar said never do a good deal with a bad guy. Some of the best advice I have ever received.

Persistence is more important than talent.

It takes time to create anything of value. As Jim would say, give yourself the gift of patience and time.

Always think outside the box. I'm a contrarian by nature. I look for how to make something better.

Discover your secret sauce and focus on what competitive advantage you can bring.

Be a student and always be learning. But as Jim says, make sure every decision is the product of your own conclusion.

Ask for divine help. Faith has played a huge part of everything I've ever done. Look for the signs.

Lastly, be YOU. When you focus on being your best self and not someone else, that is when your true genius starts to shine.

I will leave you with Jim Rohn's encouragement to me. He would always say, Kyle, let's do something remarkable!

Yes, let's do something remarkable!

Much love! Kyle

TWEETABLE

Be YOU. When you focus on being your best self and not someone else, that is when your true genius starts to shine.

Kyle Wilson, Founder of Jim Rohn International, YourSuccessStore, LessonsFromNetwork.com and KyleWilson.com. Kyle has filled big event rooms and produced 100s of programs including titles by Jim Rohn, Brian Tracy, Zig Ziglar, Denis Waitley, and recently the books Passionistas, The Little Black Book of Fitness *and* Mom & Dadpreneurs. *Kyle leads the Kyle Wilson Inner Circle Mastermind and The Kyle Wilson Mentoring Group and is the author of* 52 Lessons I Learned from Jim Rohn and Other Great Legends I Promoted *and co-author of* Chicken Soup For the Entrepreneur's Soul! *Go to KyleWilson.com/ connect to download Free books and audios and to connect on social media.*

CHAPTER 2

Tame the Brain Game

Turning Your Negative Self-Talk into a Life-Changing Mission

by Jessica Rector

Three days after I broke up with my boyfriend, I woke up and the first thing I thought was I can't be pregnant.

I got a pregnancy test on the way to church, because I needed Him to watch over me. As I sat nervously in the church bathroom with the stick, I kept thinking This can't be happening.

Thirty seconds later, the results came back. Positive.

I reread the instructions. "Wait three minutes for results."

It's only been 30 seconds, so I'm going to wait all three minutes. Maybe it's like an Etch-A-Sketch where you shake it, and it disappears.

After the three minutes, I look at the stick again. Yep, it was like an Etch-A-Sketch. The line disappeared. Unfortunately, it was the wrong line. The vertical line, positive, was still there.

What? Wait. This can't be possible. How is this possible?!

As I walked briskly through the parking lot, my thoughts came as fast as tears streamed down my face. I thought my world was coming to an end. I couldn't see anything good about this situation.

This is horrible. What am I going to do? This can't be happening. My career just went up in smoke. Now I'm going to have to get a 9-5 job…and hate every minute of it. I need to call my best friend. I need to call my sister. I need to talk to someone. What in the world? This is not happening.

Once I reached my car, with my face soaked by tears, I dialed my best friend. He didn't answer. I called my sister, she didn't answer. I called my other best friend. She didn't answer. I screamed, "Can someone PLEASE answer their phone?!"

Then the real test came.

The phone rang. It was my ex. He wanted to come and get the rest of his things. On the phone, he asked me what was wrong.

I said, "I'll tell you when I see you."

Since he left one of his cars at my place, I picked him up. When he got in the car and sat down, I showed him the pregnancy test.

He said, "You probably poured Kool-Aid on it?"

I replied, "What? That's not even possible."

He said, "Well, you got what you wanted…a baby and no guy."

"Why, yes, that's every girl's dream."

"Well, we're going to have to get married."

"What?"

"I'm not having a baby out of wedlock."

I replied, "Well, it's a good thing you're not having the baby."

After seeing him a couple more times to talk things over, I never saw or heard from him again.

Outside of my family and a couple of friends, I didn't share my pregnancy with anyone. There were no exciting moments, photos shared, or revealing the gender postings on social media.

From the moment I got the news of a baby, negative thoughts continued to rush over me as though it was my norm. These thoughts told me that people would judge me. That no one would hire me if they knew I was pregnant. No one would like me or want to be my friend. And I listened to this negative self-talk…and I believed it.

Since I believed it, I allowed these thoughts to impact my actions, behaviors, and attitude. They changed how I was showing up, my confidence, and my ability to just be me. So I hid. I wore long, flowy dresses hiding my ever expanding stomach. When I'd go out in public, I wouldn't look people in the eyes, scared they'd see this secret I was trying to desperately to hide.

The closer I got to delivery, the more, little by little, I allowed myself to get excited about my baby. To see the good, the positive, and the blessing of my baby. I began to let the hurt and pain dissipate and love and acceptance enter, and that is where things really changed.

At about eight months pregnant, I came out about my pregnancy through a blog. I received so much positive support and feedback that I decided to tell people about it, even though I was scared.

The first time I shared it in person, I went up to a complete stranger and said, "Hi, I haven't met you. My name is Jessica Rector."

She said, "I'm Sally Wall."

I replied, "I'm about to be a single mom."

Boom! Just like that.

She said, "I was raised by a single mom."

"I'd love to hear about that," and she continued to tell me her story.

I thought, That wasn't THAT bad. The ceiling didn't cave in. I'm still standing here and, yep (as I laid my hand on my chest), still breathing. I can do that again.

And I did. The next person was a single mom herself.

Then I did it again and again. What I found was I was so scared others would judge me that I was holding myself back in my business, in my life, and from connecting with others. My ability to be vulnerable allowed others to share their stories and be vulnerable too, and that's how we really connect as humans.

The fear I had was directly caused by the negative thoughts I had been telling myself over and over again and believing each time. If they had this strong of a hold of me and kept me captive for nine months, how else were they impacting my life?

I dove head first into my negative thoughts. How were they showing up in my life? How were they affecting my work? How did they manifest in things that seemed to be unrelated to each other?

Through this work, I had a revelation. I realized the connection between negative thoughts and shame. If not for shame, the negative thoughts would cease to exist. I was engulfed in shame around my pregnancy without ever realizing it. It was just the story I kept telling myself. I had to stop this thinking by figuring out where my shame came from and how to work through it.

Reviewing how shame had showed up over the course of my life, I knew the more I kept shame quiet, the more it grew and the more power it had to control me. And the more the negative thoughts would come, the more I would continue to believe them. It was time. I HAD to interrupt this pattern in order to stop it from growing.

This journey was muddy and icky and painful. Oh-so-painful. It was the late nights on the bathroom floor, crying the ugly cry, (where I couldn't breathe and gave myself a headache from crying so many tears) from the hurt. From feeling less than, not good enough, not worthy.

I asked myself the hard questions around my pregnancy…the tough questions like how could you let this happen? Were you that desperate for love that you were willing to overlook some truths about him until you just couldn't anymore? Why were you so desperate for someone in your life? Are you lovable? Why do you not feel worthy of love? Are you defined by being a single mom? Does that change who you are?

Some of the questions I didn't know the answers to right away. Some I did. And the honest answers were gut wrenchingly hard to face. I had never asked myself such poignant questions and never wanted the truth more than I had wanted to avoid the pain of answering those questions, which is why I had never been so honest with myself before now. Working through my shame also meant facing my fears and truth head on, which is exactly what I did.

And you know what? What I thought would happen, people not liking me, my world not being the same, or people not wanting to do business with me…none, none of that happened. In fact, talking about my shame liberated me…freed me from the life in chains I had been living: the life where I was hiding, scared to be me, scared to be seen.

It was in those painful moments that I also realized that all of those negative thoughts were just lies I told myself…because why? Because someone else might have said these things to me, and I believed them. I believed them over what I knew to be true about myself…that I am not less than, that I am good enough, that I am worthy.

No one else's opinion matters more than my own, so why was I giving them the power over me. Why was I choosing to give them the power over me?

It all begins with what you're saying to yourself about yourself. Everything must start with changing the conversations you have with yourself.

This process worked for me to change my negative thoughts and tackle shame, so I shared it with others. It worked for them. Then I developed a system and shared it on a bigger scale and found it worked for hundreds of others too.

I was on a high. Working through my negative thoughts was hard, but then something happened that made it harder.

I got the news that would forever change my life. My older brother, Jeff, who had just turned 40, killed himself.

I...JUST...NEVER...SAW...THIS...COMING

My dad didn't want me to share how my brother died with anyone. I think my dad thought it was a reflection of him. (It was a clear example of how negative thoughts can impact you and your decisions.) And I wanted to talk about Jeff and share with others how amazing he was, and I couldn't do that without sharing about how he died.

No one likes talking about suicide. No one even likes admitting they know someone who died by suicide. It's as though they will be guilty by association (i.e. they will be judged because they know someone who died by suicide).

The first time I spoke on stage publicly about negative thoughts impacting your life and mentioned the word "shame," it was in front of 5,000 men and women. I was nervous and scared, unsure how it would be received.

The most amazing thing happened after I spoke. I had both women and men share their shame stories, telling me how they need to be able to talk about this. They shared stories they had never told another person, things they had kept hidden for decades. They trusted me and felt compelled to share, and it bewildered me.

I left that conference confused. That's awesome they shared their stories, but why?

Two weeks later, as I was driving, it dawned on me. If Jeff had a safe place where he could share what was really going on in his head, maybe, just maybe things would've been different. I was determined that my brother wouldn't die in vain...that something bigger needed to come out of it.

A few months later, I met with a highly successful speaker friend. He and I were going over my speaking platform, and he asked me, "If you could have one more conversation with your brother, what would you say? What would you talk about?"

I replied, "I'd ask him, 'What are you saying to yourself. Why do you doubt yourself? What are the voices in your head telling you? Why are you second guessing yourself?' Then I would share with him all the strategies to change these things. Because these are the things that were holding him back. These are the things that were getting in the way of his joy, happiness, fun… These were getting in the way of his recognizing his value."

After that conversation, I knew that's what I needed to do. I needed to have conversations with audiences about these negative inner dialogues they have with themselves and how that self-talk holds them back. Because if this could happen to a highly successful, confident, charismatic, likable man, like my brother, it could happen to anyone.

So I conducted my own research, got statistics to back up what I already thought, and started speaking at larger conferences, companies, and organizations on improving performance, increasing sales, and enhancing influence by changing what you say to yourself about yourself. I started using what I'd say to my brother to dramatically impact individual and business effectiveness. I was using it in a bigger way to help more people.

About two weeks before my brother's birthday, a song that reminded me of him came on the radio as I was driving. That song went off, and for some reason, I couldn't stop thinking about Jeff. The more I thought about him, the sadder I got. The more I cried, the angrier I got. I got home and put on a happy face for my son. But by the time I was getting in the shower that night, I lost it.

In the bathroom, the tears kept coming. The endless conversations with Jeff wouldn't stop. I was mad. How could you do this? Why did you do this? I'm so angry at you. This makes no sense. Why aren't you here? I miss you.

My son came in the bathroom and asked, "Mama, what's taking so long for you to take a shower?"

I looked at the clock. It had been two hours, and I hadn't even gotten in the shower. I realized I had never given myself the time, space, and permission to really grieve Jeff. I was too busy taking care of my then infant son.

I needed to feel and process my emotions. They had been bottling up inside, and this was my meltdown.

My breakdown about Jeff spurred something else in me. When I had attempted suicide at 17-years-old, Jeff, who had been a freshman at college during the attempt said, "Don't ever do that again. I'm here for you, even if I'm at college."

He helped me feel safe…loved…wanted…needed. Something I wasn't getting from others in my life at that time. And then, ironically, he took himself away from me in that same manner he warned me against. And, it hurt.

But this breakdown was exactly what I needed to talk about me. To talk about the negative thoughts that led to my own suicide attempt. I had somehow forgotten about this. Outside of my family, over the course of 23 years, I had only told two other people. I thought I had done all the shame work, yet I was unknowingly still living in shame around this. So I started sharing it.

I shared it loudly. I shared it to give myself a voice. I shared it to help others. I shared it for Jeff. I shared it to stop hiding. I shared it to be vulnerable. I shared it to be authentic. I shared it for me. Because "Those who mind don't matter, and those who matter don't mind," from Dr. Seuss.

And by sharing it, I not only gave myself a louder, bigger voice, but I also liberated myself from all the fears, shame, and negative thoughts that still had their claws in me. I gave myself freedom without realizing that's what I craved and desired the most.

My negative thoughts, my single mom shame, and the shame around suicide (Jeff's and my attempt) were the catalysts for writing my #1 best-selling book Breaking the Silence: Taking the Sh(hh) Out of Shame. I wrote this book to help others battle their shame, so they can step into more freedom to love, succeed, learn, connect, and grow in life and business. In it, I share with you the five step process that helped me and hundreds of others walk through their shame.

Because of this process, I'm now able to present more confidently on stages around the world helping others to overcome and overhaul their inner dialogue. I also know firsthand the impact of negative thoughts (i.e. brain games) and the solutions needed to change them, which allows me to work more effectively with companies in consulting and training their people to Tame the Brain Game, providing quicker results and dramatically improving their business.

Shame spurs the negative thoughts which kill your confidence, prohibit you from taking action, and keep you from achieving all you want.

The more you talk about it, the less power and control it has over you. Free yourself from what holds you back by changing your internal conversations.

Use your negative thoughts for something bigger. Turn them into positive action. When you do this, you'll eradicate the negative inner dialogue, step more confidently in your power, and achieve everything you want!

TWEETABLE

80% of your thoughts are negative. Tame the Brain Game you're having with yourself. Turn your negative self-talk into positive action.

As an award-winning former top sales leader at a Fortune 100 company, #1 best-selling author of Breaking the Silence: Taking the Sh(hh) Out of Shame. Jessica Rector works with organizations to Tame the Brain Game and improve performance, sales, and influence.

Jessica transforms lives through consulting, training, and speaking. Some of her clients include American Airlines, Keller Williams, Sales 3.0 Conference, and American Veterinary Medical Association.

Jessicarector.com
jessica@jessicarector.com
(817) 523-1529

CHAPTER 3

The First Step to Success

by Pat Rigsby

A journey of a thousand miles begins with a single step.
— **Lao Tzu**

Do you have a goal that you want to pursue?

Are you finding it difficult to take that first step toward making this goal a reality?

What's holding you back?

What has stopped you from taking those first steps to success?

Here are a few obstacles that have affected me at one time or another in the past:

Feeling Overwhelmed. Read the Lao Tzu quote again: "A journey of a thousand miles begins with a single step."

No matter how large or how small the endeavor, you still have to begin with a single action. You don't have to have it all figured out. Simply take the first step.

Fear of _____. (Fill in the blank.) It could be any number of things.

Failure. Humiliation. Loss.

Odds are the fear that you're experiencing is far worse than the actual reality of if whatever you're afraid of did happen. 99% of the time, the fear that's holding you back is not that big of a deal. The potential discomfort you'd experience is nothing compared to the elation you'd experience from actually achieving your goal.

Unwilling to Leave the Comfort Zone. This is just a nicer way of saying you're being too lazy to reach your goals.

You must accept that achieving anything of significance requires work and dedication. So logout of Facebook, quit texting, hop off the couch, and make your dreams happen.

Comparing Yourself with Others. Your objectives should simply be tied to reaching your own potential.

Don't worry about other people and what they've done unless it fuels you to work harder and do more. Otherwise, focus on being the best version of you.

Thinking Things Had to Be Perfect. Waiting until the situation is perfect is a direct route to inaction because the situation will never be perfect.

No matter how well prepared you are, there will always be something unexpected that pops up, so don't let the need for perfection stand in your way.

Doing More Research. This is just another way of saying you're too lazy to do the real work.

As I just mentioned, things don't have to be perfect to get started, so the need for endless research before taking action is completely unfounded.

Not Feeling "Worthy" Enough. Not believing that you had enough education, knowledge, skill, or experience can stop you before you get started, but the truth is that you can't get experience without "doing" and you can't develop your skill without practice.

Most every "expert" I know felt this way at one point or another and still proceeded to take action. So should you.

If you're like me, the six things that I listed above have at one time or another stood between inaction and action. But they're all just small obstacles designed to separate the haves from the have-nots, the successful from the average. The real bottom line is this: no matter what your goal is, the best time to start is now.

I learned this back when I became a college baseball coach at the ripe old age of 23. At that point I was the youngest collegiate head coach in the country and felt a version of all seven things I listed previously.

Becoming a head coach was completely overwhelming for someone who'd just graduated college a few months before. Being responsible for over 30 young men and a collegiate athletic program was far more responsibility than I'd ever had before.

I was afraid of failure and humiliation. The program had never had a winning season prior to my taking over in spite of being led by two well-known and previously successful coaches, so the odds were stacked against me, and I was worried about doing so poorly that I'd be fired and ruin any chance of getting another job in coaching.

It's easy to say, "I'd like to be a college coach" but actually stepping up and applying and potentially being rejected was something that I struggled with.

I looked at all the coaches of the programs I'd be coaching against, and it was obvious that they were far more experienced, more knowledgeable, and had superior resources. I also took notice of the two previous coaches who'd held the position that I was applying for and recognized that, by most any standard, they were far superior to me as a coach.

I knew that the circumstances I was potentially entering were not ideal. A program with poor resources, a limited budget, and no track record of success wasn't exactly the ideal launching pad for a successful career.

Most 23-year-olds that were interested in being a baseball coach were taking positions as assistant coaches for high school JV teams, not going after collegiate head coaching jobs. Why should I be any different?

But, ultimately, I accepted the premise above: the best time to start is now.

And I learned as I went.

When I started coaching, I didn't know how to run a practice, how to motivate players, or how to recruit effectively.

But I accepted the challenge and started the job anyway.

The first few months were really tough.

After my first season I still hadn't "found myself" as a coach.

We had a winning season (barely), the first in school history in my first year, but it was more of a throwing-stuff-against-the-wall-to-see-what-sticks approach than actually figuring things out.

Thankfully, the experience taught me a lot. The next year the team did better. By the third season we were nationally ranked, and in the fifth season we finished fifth at the World Series.

And none of this would have happened unless I took the first step in spite of my insecurities.

And what I learned through that experience has benefited me time and time again.

No matter what your goal, success is a process, and it requires overcoming limiting beliefs and taking action.

Maybe your goal is to finally start your business.

Perhaps it's to launch a business online or perhaps to write a book.

Maybe your goals are to get to $500,000 in business revenue or $100,000 in personal income.

It really doesn't matter whether you want to start a business or grow one. Whether you want to create a product or write a best-seller.

Actually, I'd encourage you to dream big and set lofty goals for yourself. That's part of what makes life worth living.

But you must understand, the key isn't so much what the goal is, but how you act on it.

Once you've set your goal, big or small, you will do much, much better if you spend more time thinking about your first steps than just the big picture dreams and goals that you've laid out.

Just recently while doing a coaching session with a client of mine, I suggested that in addition to the big dreams he had set out for himself, he might also benefit from having some realistic goals for the short term.

I then proceeded to suggest a few.

While I don't know your particular "big goals," here are a few example first step goals that will help you generate momentum and start making real progress toward where you want to be:

If you want to launch a product, consider setting a filming date and hiring a videographer.

If you want to write a book, begin with writing 500 words a day.

If you want to take 100 days off next year, start by scheduling a vacation or at least a long weekend.

If you want to go from a personal income of $50,000 a year to $100,000 a year, commit to adding $500 in monthly income in the coming month.

To someone who is where you want to go, these kinds of goals might seem rather small and insignificant—but to get the momentum you need to succeed they'd be a good start.

To get to your big dreams there are a lot of steps in between.

And many of those steps might not be as exciting or as fun to think about as the big endpoint you've identified as your ideal destination. But often it's important to focus on the very next steps that you need to take in order to move towards your goals.

This is how you generate momentum.

By putting one foot in front of the other.

By getting one new client.

By writing a newsletter to your subscribers even when taking an hour to check Facebook sounds far better.

Success isn't a big leap.

It's the combination of hundreds or even thousands of little steps in succession.

But most people don't recognize that, so they look for the magic bullet.

The quick fix.

And while this isn't good news if you're looking for immediate gratification, it's great news if you're willing to start stepping.

Because you understand that the magic is in the process and the process begins with that first step.

And don't think that you're stuck taking what you may feel are baby steps for long. Once you've achieved these first small goals, start to increase them.

You might want to go from taking that long weekend to a full vacation or from adding $500 in monthly income to $1000.

Before you know it, you've put a series of steps together and you're well on your way to achieving your big goal.

But before you can run, you need to walk.

To quote Dr. Denis Waitley, "There never was a winner who was not first a beginner."

The most important thing you can do to make your goals a reality is that first step.

TWEETABLE

"No matter what your goal, success is a process and it requires overcoming limiting beliefs and taking action."
— Pat Rigsby

Pat Rigsby is an entrepreneur and business coach. He has built over 25 businesses including multiple-time winners on the Entrepreneur Franchise 500 and a multiple time honoree on the Inc. 5000.

He has also authored 11 books and has been featured in Entrepreneur, Forbes, Men's Health, USA Today, *and on hundreds of other media outlets.*

You can learn more about Pat and subscribe to his daily Ideal Business Newsletter at www.PatRigsby.com.

CHAPTER 4

Killer Confidence: Ditch the Self Doubt

Walk into Any Room with Confidence!

by Diane Consolino

A s my client's eyes unexpectedly brimmed with tears, she slowly shook her head in disbelief. She never thought that the sad story she was telling would be her own.

She is successful. She is smart. She is clever. She is a high achiever. How could this be happening to her at this point in her career?

From the outside looking in, her life looked great. Nobody would ever guess that she had a lack of self-confidence. But the truth was she could not eliminate the self doubt that repeatedly played in the back of her mind.

These thoughts were causing too much stress. Too much indecision. Too much overwhelm. Too much demand to be perfect. Too many feelings of not good enough. And they were stealing her results and her happiness.

This story is not unusual. These feelings are not unusual. Working with smart, successful, high achieving women from all over the country, I regularly hear similar experiences.

Self doubt seldom announces itself. It always slips in like a silent thief. It is sneaky, showing itself quietly in the form of hesitation, questioning your decisions, and feeling like a fraud. Unknowingly, bit by bit, self doubt is like a thief that steals your confidence and leaves you questioning yourself and your life.

I understood her pain. I understood her tears. Her story had, once upon a time, been my life. My client was in the perfect place, because I had the solution to her problems.

Let's start at the beginning...
As I lay in my bed hopelessly praying for sweet teenage dreams, my parents voices float up from the downstairs kitchen table, flooding my bedroom. The argument was always the same.

My father's voice filled with disdain and anger of my failure to live up to his expectations.

My mother's voice filled with desperation trying to defending her daughter.

My heart filled with confusion and torment as tears rolled down my cheeks soaking my pillow.

I felt confused by his anger toward me. I was confused by his disdain toward me. I was tormented by the idea that no matter how hard I worked or how much I achieved, my father would not love me.

I tried relentlessly to win his approval. In high school I was a top female athlete, lettering my freshman through senior years. Throughout high school I was on the honor roll and a member of both the band and choir. I never broke curfew or partied. I was a rule follower and desperate for his love.

The constant criticism from my father started to strip away my natural confidence, and I began to second guess all my decisions. The constantly watching, editing, and managing myself as I tried desperately not to make mistakes was exhausting.

Outwardly I tried my best to appear confident and outgoing. Looking back, I can see that instead of confident, I was mostly opinionated and defensive, often holding strong to my opinion for fear that if even the smallest crack would make me look weak.

The pressure of pretending to be confident and pretending that I did not care about what other people thought was a constant balancing act, especially when the truth was that the smallest disapproval by him, by anyone, felt like my soul was being shattered.

In college, I grew tired of feeling weak and vulnerable, so I changed my strategy. Overtime I became a hard shell disguised in the body of a fun, wild party girl. Drinking heavily and partying hard between periods of depression where I could barely get myself out of bed consumed my life.

I was drowning. Drowning in the booze. Drowning in the partying. Drowning in my loneliness. Drowning in my heartbreak. Drowning in my sadness. Drowning in my not-enough-ness. But mostly, I was drowning in the fear that this torment would never leave me, and that it would forever define my life.

It was a miracle that I survived college, graduating with an accounting degree. It was an even bigger miracle that underneath all of the self-doubting and low self-esteem lived a desire to break away from the powerful undertow that was dragging me under.

Desperation mixed with desire can be a powerful motivator...

I made a plan. I got a job. I worked crazy hours. I saved money. I took graduate courses in long-term health care. I completed an internship. And before I knew it, I had loaded up my old, slightly beaten, four door, baby blue Plymouth Reliant and, for the first time in my life, was on my way to California.

I was armed with my college degree, a long-term care license, and a thousand dollars.

I was equipped with years of working hard to pay my own way.

I was motivated by the need to flee the pain that defined my life.

I was driven with the grit of a person desperate not to fail.

I was filled with hope, promise, and a vision.

And most importantly, I embraced my inner rule breaker. I had grown to understand that learning to live by my own rules was the only way that I would create the life I craved.

Within a few months I had secured a great job in a long-term care health facility as an administrator, and I had moved to an apartment by the beach. This once landlocked, drowning young woman was living a ten minute walk from the beach feeling happy and free.

It was my first job as an administrator. Although, I was well trained, I am the first to admit being well trained is not exactly the same as being skilled at the job. Luckily, I was blessed with a generous, well seasoned staff who were extremely kind and supportive.

Everyday I showed up to work with a positive attitude of gratitude to the people in my facility. Everyday I showed up to work impeccably, professionally dressed. Everyday I showed up to work ready to work hard.. Everyday I showed up to work willing to learn.

But most importantly, everyday I showed up to work determined to release a lifetime of pain and recreate a new life.

I knew that in order for my staff, the residents, and their family members to have faith in their young, new administrator it was important to present myself with confidence.

Immediately I worked on eliminating the habit of speaking about myself in a negative manner. I had grown to understand that it was hard for others to have confidence in me when I spoke poorly about myself. I watched my language and created a new habit of speaking of myself only in positive terms.

Confidence is a skillset...

When you work in a long-term health facility, one of the keys to managing effectively is walking the halls of the facility. This allows the administrator to see what is happening in the facility. But most importantly, it allowed me to create relationships with the staff, residents, and their families.

It was the same process every time. Before I left my office to tour the facility, I would take a moment and look in the mirror that was hidden behind the office door. Looking at my reflection, I would throw my shoulders back, stand tall, and imagine being a confident person. Then, and only when I felt confident, would I walk out of my office.

It is important to point out that this process was extremely different from what I had been doing in my painful past. In the past, instead of practicing confidence, I was trying not to look weak. Trying not to look weak is not the same as practicing confidence.

Trying not to look weak is the process of masking your weakness. When you mask your weakness, what you are saying to yourself is, "I am weak, but I can't let other people see that I am weak." The concentration is on weakness, not on strength.

When I started practicing confidence, the concentration was on my feeling good, being comfortable, and owning and trusting my personal gifts and talents. I moved from worrying about what others thought about me and I was concentrating on how I want to feel about myself.

In a short period of time my confidence started to grow as I walked those halls. Before long, I noticed that people were reacting to me in a way that I had seldom experienced prior to moving to California. My staff, residents, and families trusted me and believed in my leadership; their confidence in me was both palpable and powerful.

Additionally, I started to believe and trust in myself in a way that I had never experienced in my life. I started to expect good things from myself, from the people around me, and out of life. The confidence I was experiencing felt real, but most importantly it was starting to feel natural.

Although I had made great strides growing my confidence skillset, I was still having challenges. I was uncomfortable in networking and marketing meetings where the room was filled with strangers. Meetings where I perceived people to have a higher status than me, like at corporate meetings, were intimidating. I couldn't quite figure out what was missing, but that was all about to change.

Own the room...

You might laugh when you read the source of this life-changing event. It makes me smile whenever I think about the circumstances. It is a strange source for such a life-changing event, but it changed the way I walk into any and every room.

It was a boring weekday night, and I was doing some light cleaning in my apartment to pass away the time. I was kind of sort of listening to the TV playing in the background.

Kane, on the once very popular soap opera, *All My Children*. Now, if you are not familiar, Erica Kane, she was beautiful, rich, successful, sexy, charming, and always got her man. She was also cunning, devious, divisive, manipulative, and often ruthless. Erica Kane was captivating. She was a woman everyone loved to hate.

I was walking through the room when the interviewer asked Lucci, "What is Erica's secret?" I slowed down wanting to listen to the answer. Lucci paused for a moment and said, "When Erica walks into a room she owns the room."

That reply literally stopped me in my tracks.

I stared at the TV. Time seemed to stand still. I could feel the molecules in my brain realign. Then with crystal clear confidence the thought, "I can do that!" jumped into my head.

And then I had a second thought that changed my life... "I was not walking into the wrong rooms. I was walking into the room wrong!"

I am not exaggerating, from that moment on, I practiced walking into a room, any room, every room, like I owned the room. The results were powerful. Work, play, life became so much more fun knowing that I could feel comfortable in any environment. My confidence soared!

My confidence skillset was becoming powerful, but I was aware that I had one remaining challenge to conquer, I still worried about other people's opinions. People's opinions can be a valuable resource. The problem arises when other people's opinions matter more than your own. I was still in a space where I regularly questioned myself based on others thoughts, and the self doubt was stressful and slowed down my results.

I was in search of an answer. The answer came to me the day after I threw a birthday party at my apartment.

Own the room like it is your birthday party...

We had invited our friends and told them they could invite whoever they wanted to the birthday party. Well, it turned out they wanted to invited a lot of their friends. As people piled into our small, now overcrowded apartment, we talked, danced, and laughed deep into the night.

The next day while I was hanging out with friends, rehashing the fun of the previous night, it occurred to me that I didn't have any hesitancy meeting or holding conversations with anyone at my party.

No matter the person's social status or profession, I greeted everyone with a smile, hugging them with complete confidence, and saying whatever I wanted to say without consideration of their opinion. If we connected, great. If we did not connect, next. There was no worrying about what they thought about me. I had complete freedom at my party.

I thought to myself, "What was the difference between this party and the times where I walk into a room and felt uncomfortable? "

All of a sudden my eyes opened wide and in that light bulb moment I found the missing link… "I should own the room like it is my birthday party!"

A thought can be powerful, but action is were the results live.

I put that thought into practice. I was intentional. I was determined. I practiced the process at work. I practiced the process at play. Whenever I walk into a room, any room, every room I practiced owning the room like it was my birthday party.

The results were amazing.

To this day, no matter the situation, if I feel my confidence wane, all I need to do is pause, throw my shoulders back, stand tall, take a deep breath, and think about owning the room like it is my birthday party, and instantly I feel powerful and confident.

The results are amazing...

As a success coach and a keynote speaker, I have created programs and have taught thousands of people throughout the country how to eliminate their self doubt and be confident in any room and in every situation.

One of my most requested keynotes includes, "Own The Room Like It Is Your Birthday." The talk is fun, full of laughs, and filled with easy take away tools that will increase confidence. It is so impactful that people often walk up to me years later with big smiles on their faces saying, "I am owning the room like it is my birthday!"

It is such a joy to hear my private clients rave about how the inner voice of self doubt has been transformed into a voice of confidence. They are excited about how they are making more money and getting better results all the while feeling less stressed and having more time to create the career and life they craved for years.

I understand their excitement. When I look back over my life, my journey, my struggles, and see the happiness and success that I have been able to achieve simply by working on confidence, I am so grateful.

Working with a wide variety of people, in my experience, even the most successful person can have moments when their confidence goes missing in action. That is simply human nature.

It is comforting to know that confidence is always within reach. All it takes is a little desire, the right tools, some practice, and before you know it you will be able to walk into any room like it is your birthday!

TWEETABLE
You aren't walking into the wrong room. You are walking into the room wrong. ~Diane Consolino

Diane Consolino is a powerhouse coach and speaker. She is most proud of what her clients say about working together…

"As a director of events and marketing, I hear and book many speakers and Diane is one of the few I continually rebook for a variety of different audiences. Her authentic personality and honesty with the crowd keeps the group captivated throughout her talks. She is hilarious and smart with such insight on her topics that everyone will find something to take away from their time with Diane. If you don't hire this funny lady for your next conference or event you are missing out!" – T. Olson

LEARN MORE: DianeConsolino.com

CONTACT: Diane@DianeConsolino.com

FACEBOOK: Diane Consolino

At DianeConsolino.com SIGN UP for Diane's FREE…5 WEEKS to KILLER CONFIDENCE PROGRAM!

CHAPTER 5

Actions Speak Louder than Words – A Lesson Learned from My Daughter

by Robert Crockett

"Actions speak louder than words" was something my father told me too many times to count when I was growing up. I've heard it said by many people. I've read it in a number of books. I remembered it, maybe even believed it, but I probably didn't live it until my daughter's 14th birthday. This is the story of how a 50-year-old man from Iowa who had never considered getting a tattoo or a body piercing ending up with a pierced ear.

The month before my daughter, Christine, turned 14, I moved out of the house into a hotel with my son, DJ, who had just turned 18. Christine, due to her age, stayed with her mother. As sometimes happens when a family starts to tear apart, and through no one's fault, I couldn't see my daughter from the day we moved until her birthday. It was the longest period we had been apart, and for me it was crushing.

DJ and I went to pick up Christine at her mother's house on her birthday. After we got past the initial awkwardness, which included the question, "Why did you leave me?" I told Christine we could do anything she wanted for her birthday. She smiled for the first time since we picked her up and said, "I want my nose pierced." Looking back on it, I'm impressed at how quickly she boxed me into a corner; Christine had been asking me for two years to have her nose pierced, and for two years I had been telling her no. But I had just told her she could do anything she wanted for her birthday. Ultimately, my guilt at leaving her won out, and I told her to pick a place to have it done and we would do it.

We drove to the piercing establishment and spent some time talking to the owner and picking out her new jewelry. Once we had signed the forms, we stood by the window to watch the people who were ahead of us get various parts of their bodies pierced. After watching a couple of people get their piercings I heard a sniffle behind me. I turned and looked at Christine who, with tears in her eyes said, "I changed my mind. We don't need to get my nose pierced. We can leave."

Christine had gotten her ears pierced when she was a baby, and she had never remembered experiencing any type of piercing. I knew right away she still wanted her nose pierced, but watching the other people get their piercings had scared her. I was being selfish, but now it was important to me that Christine get her nose pierced. I needed something she would remember to offset what had happened in the last month. She was next in line; I walked over to the owner and told him my daughter was scared and asked would they pierce my ear first so she could see that it didn't hurt. I told Christine I was getting my ear pierced, and we could either leave after I was done or she could get her nose pierced. I walked into the room, sat down, and looking at my daughter the whole time, I got my ear pierced without flinching. (Of course, I know now it doesn't hurt, but at that point in my life I had no experience in having needles pushed through my body.) When I walked out, she was smiling and walked into the piercing room and had her nose pierced.

We spent the rest of an incredible day together and finally it was time to take Christine home. We dropped her off, said our goodbyes and drove back to our hotel. As soon as we got to the hotel room I pulled the earring out and put it on the night stand. DJ asked me why I took the earring out, and I told him I got my ear pierced so Christine would know that it didn't hurt, but there was no way I was showing up to work tomorrow with an earring. DJ looked at me like the fool I am and said, "You better think about that. It's important to her that you got your ear pierced and you did it together." I pretty much dismissed what he said and put the earring away without thinking about it.

It was another week before I was able to see Christine again. When I was getting ready to leave, DJ asked me about the earring. I asked him if he really thought it was important, and he said it was. Deciding to put the earring back in caused thirty minutes of chaos. First, I couldn't remember where I left it (now that I decided to put it back in, it felt more important than before). Then, when I found it, I couldn't put it in because the hole had closed. Starting to panic, I went to the front desk for a needle, but they didn't have any. As a last resort, I put the earring between my fingers, took a deep breath, and pushed it through my ear where I had gotten the piercing. That time it hurt. I recommend a professional. I wiped the blood off the back of my ear and headed off to see my daughter, only twenty minutes late.

When Christine got into the car, the first thing she did was turn my head so she could see the earring and said, "How's your earring doing?" (Yes, my kids are smarter than me.) I told her it was taking some time to get used to, but I was going to keep it.

Over the next year, Christine would look at earrings with me and, occasionally, give one to me. I knew that getting the piercing was important to her, but it wasn't until I took her to the hospital to see her mother a year later as she was coming out of surgery that I realized just how important it was. Her mother hadn't really seen Christine and I together since I had moved out, and still a little woozy from the surgery, she looked at Christine, looked at me, then back at Christine and said, "You guys have the same earrings." Christine nodded, looking at me a little sheepishly as I realized that whenever she gave me an earring, she kept the second earring and then would change her earring if I changed mine.

Years have gone by, and getting my ear pierced still comes up in conversation. We had a family reunion in Iowa earlier this summer; Christine was talking to a cousin about their nose piercings, and Christine told her cousin to ask me to tell the story about how I got my ear pierced. When I look back on that day, I could have told her that it wouldn't hurt, could have said we didn't need to do it, and we could have left. I did take an action that, to me, was all about making my daughter feel safe and happy (and making me feel better about myself). But more importantly, in my daughter's eyes, I took an action that bonded us and made her realize there isn't anything I wouldn't do for her.

Today, I truly believe actions speak more loudly than words, but it's much more important and deeper than the common saying. What's important is that not only are people watching what you do and seeing how it matches to what you say, they are also watching your actions and making judgments. We have no idea how important our actions may be to them.

TWEETABLE
Even when it doesn't seem important, people are watching your actions and making judgments.

Robert Crockett resides in Las Vegas and is the proud father of two amazing children. He has founded, managed, and reorganized numerous businesses. Today, he owns and operates Advanced Personal Care Solutions, a home health company he founded in 2004 employing over 240 employees and providing service and support to the elderly and disabled. Robert is an author, John Maxwell coach, and speaker.

Email Robert@rpcrockett.com
Website rpcrockett.com
Twitter @RobertPCrockett

CHAPTER 6

Change Is Inevitable, Choose It and Grow with It

by Felecia Froe, M.D.

'm a urologist. I've been a urologist for over 20 years. It was during the first five years that I knew that this would not be the last work that I did. When I identified a systemic issue in our current medical system, I became very passionate and I created my medical communications company, 18 Seconds for Health.

"Dad, I want to be be a veterinarian."

"If you're going to school for that long, you are going to be a doctor."

From that day forward, I was going to medical school. I don't remember the feeling of wanting to be a veterinarian. I remember really liking animals. My father was a veterinarian. It just seems like when he said it, it was true. I was in junior high, so I had a few years of school to get through. The rest of junior high and high school went by fairly uneventfully. Then came college. You see, I was a pretty "controlled" kid in high school. I went in to college majoring in biology. The classes were HARD and I wanted to have a good time, and I did. That was when others, like college counselors and friends started telling me that maybe I wasn't meant for medical school. I was told that I would never make it. I was also having my own doubts. How could I do that and get married and have kids? I just couldn't see it.

I ended up in St. Louis at the pharmacy school. I took a bus from Kansas City to St. Louis with all of my stuff for the year. I was a good pharmacy student. I made friends and joined the pharmacy fraternity. Pharmacy school was challenging, but boring. After a while, I was having a hard time seeing myself as one of those people behind a counter counting pills. While in school, I worked in a hospital pharmacy. There you had to think. We compounded drugs, mixed chemotherapy medications, and calculated doses. I thought, maybe I could do this, but I would need to be a PharmD— that's a pharmacy doctor (yeah, I didn't know it existed either).

One night I was working at the pharmacy, and there was a code blue. One of my best friend's brother was in the hospital, and the code was on his floor. Lots of people started coming to the pharmacy to get different drugs that they needed for the code. Somehow I found out that it was him. He had sickle cell and was in the hospital a lot. After the flow of people slowed, I got to go upstairs to check on him. There was a doctor sitting at a desk. I asked, "How's Andy?"

He shook his head with a look that said everything, "He didn't make it." The tears welled up in my eyes and rolled down my face. The pain of that moment was so intense. I remember thinking of my friend. After I called my mother to help to calm me down, I called my friend. The first thing, she yelled, "MY BROTHER IS DEAD!" My composure was gone.

I went to his funeral and hung around with my friend for a while, preoccupied with the knowledge that I had to do something else with my life. I was bored. Pharmacy was not for me. I think this was my first glimpse at how short life really is.

I told my father that I wanted to go to medical school. He was not for it at all. He thought that I should finish pharmacy, work for a while, and then if I still wanted to, I could go to medical school. He had my cousin call me to talk to me about it. I talked to medical school admissions counselors who said that it would be unlikely that I got accepted out of pharmacy school. I was told that professional schools did not take each other's students.

I decided I was going to go to medical school. I checked out the curriculum of my college to see what degree I could get the fastest given the credits that I already had. I could get a BA in Chemistry in a year. I took care of that real quick and I transferred out of pharmacy school.

I applied to quite a few medical schools, and one by one I got my rejection letters. One evening I was in my chemistry lab, I looked up and saw my family in the hallway. The first thing I thought was "Who died?" They were all there, weird. I went into the hallway and my dad handed me a thick envelope from the University of Missouri School of Medicine. It was like slow motion. I opened the letter—I WAS ACCEPTED. I'm going to medical school! I'm going to get to be a pediatrician, or family doctor, or geriatrician. We were so happy.

Medical school was tough. Everyone helped each other. We worked hard. The first two years are like regular college: you go to class, you sit, you listen, you take tests. The third and fourth years are "rotations." This is where you get to try on the different specialties. We learned to talk to patients, to understand why they came to the doctor, figure out how to help them. We learned how to examine patients, order tests and find the abnormalities, and talk about how to correct the problems.

After doing several rotations, I was panicked because the things that I thought I would like, I hated. Pediatrics and internal medicine were not for me. Surprisingly, I really liked the surgical subspecialties and settled on urology. When I let that cat out of the bag, one of the women general surgeons told me that I wouldn't make it as a urologist. By now, I had figured out that all I needed to get something done was for someone to tell me that I couldn't.

I am in my 24th year of being a urologist. I realized in the first five years that medicine as it is practiced today is not for me. As I have continued to practice, I have come to understand why. I learned to ask questions in medical school, to interview a patient. I realize now that I always expected a patient to be able to tell me what I need to know. One of my mentors actually told me that if I asked the right questions, listened, really listened to the answers, the patient would give me their diagnosis. It was true. In medical school, it was true. Yes, tests did need to be ordered to confirm, but usually, the patient could tell you the diagnosis.

What was different out of medical school? Time was different. In medical school, I was given time to develop my technique of asking questions and listening to answers. In the "real world," I did not have the luxury of so much time. In the "real world" time is money. The more time I spent with a patient, the fewer patients I could see. The fewer patients I could see, the less money I made for myself and the group. I learned that medicine is a business. Without making money to pay the staff, to pay the rent, to buy the supplies, we could not stay in business.

Due to continued changes in the "healthcare" system, the cost of running the business continued to increase, while payment for the product, healthcare, continued to decrease. The only way to keep up was to spend less time with each patient. Patients did not know this, they did not understand. I did not have time to get you, the patient, to give me the answers, to tell me the diagnosis. Especially when most of you came in ill-prepared to answer the questions.

During this time, I read Robert Kiyosaki's book *Rich Dad Poor Dad*. I saw that there was a different way to bring value to the world, by building a business. I learned that entrepreneurs solve problems. I also learned about real estate investing. I continued my education in entrepreneurship and real estate while I continued with my urology practice. The problem that I see is two-fold. Too many patients have no idea how to talk to their doctor and do not take responsibility for their health and too many people take no responsibility for their financial health. Too many people turn their physical and financial health over to someone else.

18 Seconds for Health was born to help patients communicate better with their doctor. Studies have shown that your doctor will interrupt you within 18 seconds of you starting to talk. 18 Seconds for Health is to prepare you for the conversation, to help you make the most of those first seconds to help your doctor to understand.

Narwhal Investment Group was born to help accredited investors achieve equity growth, passive income and tax benefits while maintaining privacy through real-estate related private placement offerings. We seek projects that will add value to the community in which we are investing.

I am a teacher, I've been doing it for 24 years: working to get people to understand, working to get them to take responsibility, teaching them how to ask questions, to trust their instincts.

I have learned that I am not comfortable being comfortable. I love to do new things, scary things, things people say that I cannot do. Fortunately, I do not hang around too many people with those kind of limiting beliefs. My friends push me, encourage me, and tell me that I can do anything. I am doing things that I never knew about 20 years ago. I am teaching people how to invest their money in real assets, working to help them be responsible for their wealth and health.

I am a strategic health and wealth educator whose mission is to help people become responsible for their health and wealth.

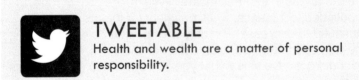

TWEETABLE
Health and wealth are a matter of personal responsibility.

Dr. Felecia Froe is a practicing urologist in California. She has two companies, 18 Seconds for Health and Narwhal Investment Group. 18 Seconds for Health is her medical communication company. Her mission is to help improve the current health care system by helping patients communicate more clearly with their doctors. Having practiced medicine for 24 years, she is uniquely qualified to pull back the curtain so that the general public can know how to help their doctor help them.

Narwhal Investment Group works with accredited investors to help them gain control and understanding of the investing process. Her mission is to help people become as responsible for their wealth as she wants them to be for their health.

Health and wealth are both a matter of personal responsibility.

feleciafroemd@gmail.com
feleciafroemd.com
narwhalinvestmentgroup.com

CHAPTER 7

Bold Decisions
The Power of Our Environment
by Marc-Andre Gagnon

Sweaty palms, butterflies, fast heart beat! What did I get myself into!? Less than 15 minutes earlier, I was outside laughing with my parents, proud and happy to be here. Then a senior officer cadet told us: officer cadets need to come inside so we can show them to their rooms. We all started walking, or I should say, straying like a herd of cattle, and as the last person entered the building, "CLANG." The 12-foot door was slammed shut and all hell broke loose. Life as I knew it, would be no more for the next weeks and months...orders were coming left and right. No talking. Stand properly. Look forward. One by one, our rights were being pulled away. The right to talk, there will be no talking unless you are asked a question; the right to walk freely, when inside or outside, you will walk in a straight line, eyes forward, arms balancing; and when crossing the parade square, you will run at all times. You are not allowed to go outside unless told. You cannot leave the campus, nor call anyone, nor write to anyone (no cell phone or computers in those days, so we could not cheat). You cannot wear any civilian clothes. Showers will be with cold water only, and will be for a max of three minutes and you will use shampoo and soap and rinse within those three minutes.

How did I get there? Well, by my own choosing.

When reading the above, I know many people are thinking as my kids tell me: why would I want to go through this? I understand because the same question crossed my mind many times. I also had this thought many times when going through boot camp, but after I completed it and ever since then, I can say without a doubt that this was one of the most important turning points of my life. It allowed me to change the direction of my life by completely changing my environment. I moved into an environment totally focused on leadership and growth.

Why was changing my environment so important?

Over the course of my schooling, I pretty much always excelled academically, but until high school I was never good at sports and was tagged as somewhat nerdy. In high school, I finally discovered my first sports passion, basketball, and this passion was the first time in my life that I had the "no matter what" mindset. I wanted to play basketball badly and nothing was going to stop me, and I succeeded and made the starting line-up in my second year of high school.

But with high school also came the need for social recognition which at times had me assert myself through making crazy and unhealthy choices like alcohol, breaking the rules, late partying, and neglecting academic work. And this approach worsened in my senior year. Throughout high school, my life revolved around basketball, and at the beginning of my senior high school year the varsity basketball program was cut due to lack of funding. I lost what was then my main passion. Basketball was my life in high school. With basketball, 90% of my non-school time was spent in the gym. Without it, much of my non-school time was now spent hanging out, free flowing or partying late, staying up until the wee hours of the night and walking into school like a zombie in the morning.

One of the challenges when we lack goals is that we become free flowing and our destination becomes highly influenced by the environment we spend time in. In my senior year, I still had big dreams for my life, but I started spending too much time with people who did not have the same level of dreams and aspiration as I had, and I was slowly settling within the confine of my social environment and could see my dreams start to fade away.

Partying and free flowing was fun and easy, but I was not happy and I was not headed where I wanted to go. Somehow, I knew I had to make a decision to start making different choices if I was going to reach my dreams and create the life I wanted.

From a very young age, my parents had planted the seed of attending the Royal Military College of Canada (RMC). It was their dream, but in my senior year, I slowly realized that it was also a path to a better and more purposeful life, and in my senior year I decided to act on this seed. I went to a recruiting center, and started the application process to attend RMC. I did not know if I could make it as the selection process was harsh, lengthy, and challenging, but fortunately, I made it through.

Needless to say, at the time, I did not really know what I was committing to. None of the new military academy movies had been made yet. But now there I was, in my first day of recruit boot camp partly wishing I was somewhere else and seriously doubting my decision. The first week was brutal: little sleep, gruesome mental challenges, and intense physical training.

Three important factors helped me make it through. First was the environment which was extremely conducive to growth and change—an environment of high achievers who for the most part had goals and were determined to achieve them. Secondly, my desire to explore the world and thirdly my competitiveness fueled me and made quitting a non-viable option.

The journey was long, challenging, filled with rollercoaster emotions, successes, failures, and lots of learnings and growth, but I made it through and graduated with an engineering degree and received my commission as an Naval Officer. But more importantly, my time at RMC established a foundation for my life and taught me many invaluable leadership and life principles.

Let me share three of those principles which I call the 3 C's of creating a desired outcome.

Clarity:
This is the starting point of realizing any dream or goal. Lack of clarity or confusion in what we want leads to daily decisions and choices which are not congruent with our wants or goals. Before I attended RMC, I had dreams and things I wanted to accomplish, but during my years at RMC I learned the power of vision and how setting clear and defined goals impacts daily decisions. Over time, the compound effect of our daily choices and decisions is what determines the life we have.

Confidence:
We are much more capable and we have much more potential than we can ever imagine. One of my mentors taught me the difference between our limits and our limitations. Our limits are set by laws such as the law of gravity and the laws of physics, but the boundaries of our achievements are most of the time determined by our limitations, which are set by what we believe we can do and achieve. The best way to build our confidence is to step outside our comfort zone into an environment which stretches us beyond our believed limitations.

Commitment:
Sustained commitment requires a mindset of "NO MATTER WHAT." To establish that mindset, we have to have clarity, confidence, and a very strong "WHY" for our goals and dreams. The most important lesson I learned about commitment is that there is no power in commitment to the destination. We have to commit to the journey, the day to day, which will eventually lead us to the destination. Many people are in love with the targeted results, but they quit before reaching the destination because they never commit to what it takes to achieve the results: commitment to making daily choices and decisions which are congruent and aligned to creating

the desired outcome. A great example is how our morning intentions fade so quickly when life happens.

The application of those leadership principles served me well during the course of my life and even more so when I decided to start my own business.

My decision to start my own business was driven by three factors: my passion for leadership, my commitment to philanthropy, and my desire to have more flexibility to spend time with my family. When I started, I had a clear vision of the life I wanted to create, but I lacked clarity on my business model. Lack of clarity made it really hard to develop a business strategy which would focus my decisions and actions on what it would take to create the business results I wanted. And lack of business results then impacted my confidence and beliefs that I could build the kind of business which would create the life I wanted. Ultimately, my doubt began to impact my commitment to the journey of building my business, to what it would take on a daily basis. This lead me to direct my focus to philanthropy and to acquiring more knowledge, thinking that more knowledge would help.

Knowledge is great, but knowledge is not necessarily learning without action, and more specifically, without a good strategy and plan, knowledge becomes a never-ending academic spiral, which in most cases leads to either never achieving our desired results or quitting.

Although the 3 C's, clarity, confidence, and commitment, allowed me to develop powerful vision, strategy, and plans to build, grow, and successfully lead many organizations in the corporate world, as a solo entrepreneur I was missing two critical ingredients to achieve the same results.

First, I was missing a community of support: people who I could brainstorm with and bounce ideas off of, people whose experience I could benefit from, people with differing viewpoints, and people who could keep me accountable to my plans. Working in large corporations, I was able to build such a group of advisors from within the organization, the environment I was working in every day, but as a solopreneur, I had to find and create this environment with other business owners and entrepreneurs. And my breakthrough came when I joined masterminds with other business owners and leaders.

One of my passions in life is wine, so I like to use many analogies using reference to winemaking. In wine making, there are three main factors that determine the quality of a wine: the grapes, the environment (climate), and the winemaker. Like grapes in a vineyard, we are not free to choose the environment we come from, but as people many of us are blessed with the freedom and power to change our environment. Changing our environment, especially the people we live with and spend time with, is one of the best ways to extend our limitations. Jim Rohn said: we become the average of the five people we spend the most time with. In my senior high school year, I was faced with two choices, settle for the life I had or make the decision to move into an environment more conducive to growth and realizing my dreams. Making the decision to change my environment was one of the most impactful decisions in my life. I believe it created the biggest turning point in my life.

Wine makers create some of the best wines through blending of different grapes. My second breakthrough came from the blending of my different passions. Working with my friend and mentor, Kyle Wilson, I realized that although I love leadership, I needed to add an ingredient to steer my passion to teach, speak, and mentor on leadership, and this ingredient came through my passion for wine. This led me to develop leadership workshops using wine making analogies to teach and demonstrate leadership principles.

From there, I started creating environments designed to nurture success through powerful business development communities for executives, leaders, business owners, and new entrepreneurs, using the concept of masterminds. If you've ever tried to learn a new language, you know that the most effective way is through immersion. The same principle applies to our personal and business growth. The level and speed of our growth and achievements are greatly influenced and empowered by our environment.

If you are seeking personal growth, building a business, or looking to transition in your life, I invite you to join me in a journey of discovery, growth, and transformation. Join our mastermind community and experience the power of mastermind and spending time with a community of like-minded people.

TWEETABLE

Commitment to a goal is the starting point. Commitment to the journey, to doing what we have to do daily, leads to amazing results.

Marc-Andre Gagnon is certified John Maxwell speaker, coach and leadership trainer, and owner of FromWhat2Why, a company which creates powerful environments for business owners, executives, and entrepreneurs to create outstanding results in their life and business. Prior to starting his business, Marc-Andre was a corporate entrepreneur who built and led organizations across multiple countries and continents for 30 years, spending some time living in Europe and Asia. He is a graduate of the Royal Military College of Canada. If you want to experience the power of many, contact marc-andre@fromwhat2why.com or LinkedIn at https://tinyurl.com/marc-andre-linkedin.

CHAPTER 8

Never Too Young to Overcome

by Freddy Perez

My father would always say, "Dime con quién andas y te diré quién eres." I remember it like it was yesterday. In English, the saying is the same as birds of a feather flock together. It's hard to argue against the evidence that has time and time again proved this saying to be true. I preach its lessons as life-creating or life-threatening. In my life, it has been one of the deciding factors in why, although still broken and searching for meaning, I find myself confident and able to share my life-defining moment with you.

I have always enjoyed performing. Maybe not in formal arenas, but I have always felt like the world is my stage. I was born the ninth of ten kids in Tamazula, Jalisco in Mexico on August 9th, 1976. At the age of three, my parents decided to bring us to this wonderful country I proudly call home. We embarked on a two-day bus ride from Tamazula to Tijuana. During that bus ride, I would play my little guitar and sing at all the stops and collect tips. Those tips would feed all of us every time we made a stop for food. My sister just posted about that trip on Facebook and although I don't really remember it, it brought tears to my eyes. There were plenty of other times that even though I was young, I knew I had to step up and did so with a confidence that only a child who truly knows he was loved could.

I was seven years old, and breakdancing was the big thing back then, at least it was in the small town called Lindsay in California's beautiful San Joaquin Valley. I was the youngest kid in our "crew," and so they would take me everywhere, and we would compete against other crews from other towns. They called me "Baby Rock." That's right, I was on the scene way before Kid Rock. A couple of years went by, and I became better and a bigger part of what we were doing.

By the time I got to fourth grade, the breakdancing climate changed. I remember we were at a park for an Easter celebration and one of our crew members got stabbed with a knife by a member of the crew which had just lost to us in the competition, also known as a battle. My mother and two of my brothers were there also and witnessed the entire thing. When we got home that night, my mother expressed her concerns with me being in that environment and I assured her it would be ok. Plus, I was growing now and felt I was gaining more influence. I couldn't stop now, I was moving up in a movement that was getting more and more popular.

Just a few years earlier, our crew started dancing and hanging out in front of the local arcade. At first we were just having fun, nothing crazy. However, by this time, we were starting to steal from stores, carry knives, and bully other kids. Some of my friends even sniffed White Out in a bag to get high. I knew what we were up to was wrong but I kept my mouth shut and went with the flow.

Gangs started infiltrating the schools, and in Lindsay we had one major one that was mostly made up of young men in their early twenties and high schoolers. They were called "The Bad Boys." The next level down was the "Future Bad Boys," mostly junior high kids. And finally you had the "Little Futures" who were middle school kids. That's right, I said middle school. You see, for those of you that have never had someone explain to you how it works, the recruiting process gangs use is one of the most sophisticated and effective ways to get people to buy into a system, way of life, or philosophy, ever created. They start early, and they go hard!

There were two brothers that were the most influential in the crew I rolled with. One was a freshman in high school, I believe, but his younger brother was my age and at the time he was my best friend. I would spend the night at his house a lot of weekends with little or no supervision. My parents had plenty of other children, most in their teens, that they had to worry about, so getting lost in the shuffle and doing my own thing was normal. On one of those weekend nights the true test came calling. I remember the older ones in the crew talking about whether they thought I was tough enough and whether I was "down." You see, the word "down" means whether you've got what it takes to be worthy of their friendship and protection, whether you will step up and be loyal or you buckle under pressure and be a liability for the rest of the crew. Weakness is not an option.

We had been scouting a home that seemed mostly abandoned. We peeked in one of the windows during the day and noticed a fully furnished but barely lived in room near the back. That same night, as we gathered down the street from the home, the time had come. They sent me to go with one of the older guys to break in and take anything we could find. He was to make sure I did this right and didn't get caught. This was the test. I was about to be 11 years old and junior high was only a year or so away. They knew I had leader qualities but they needed to know if I had what it took to be a "Future Bad Boy."

60

As we removed the screen and climbed in through the window, we noticed a VCR (actually, a Betamax) sitting on top of an old TV console. I started to unplug it from the big TV and the wall when we saw the door open and the light turn on. It was the lady. She must have been 80 years old. She dropped something she had in her hand and yelled "Get out, help, help!" The guy I was with pushed her. She hit her head on the drywall and fell to the ground. She kept yelling, "Get out! Help! Help!" I handed the Betamax to another crew member waiting outside the window, and we both jumped out. We had about 4-5 other guys waiting for us in the back alley. We all ran down that alley and high-fived each other as we laughed and mocked the scared old lady. We gathered back at one of the older guy's house and handed the loot to him. He congratulated us and gave me the look that I had wanted for so long but was now regretting. I had now proven myself and was finally considered "down."

When I got home I did what I have always done and still do to this day, I told my mother EVERYTHING. From my first kiss, to my first hit of marijuana, to the first time I had sex, I have always run to her for comfort, acceptance, and forgiveness. We stayed up for two hours, and I told her exactly what happened. She patiently listened and then passionately instructed me to not hang out with them ever again. That was easier said than done, but if mom said It, I was doing it. My mother was an extremely tough, no bullshit kind of woman. She never learned to read or write, but she knew more about life and about survival that anyone I have ever met. I guess with never making over $16,000 combined household income per year and raising 10 children...surviving is what you did.

I showed up to school on Monday a little anxious and very scared. I showed up late on purpose, and I did not come out for recess or lunch. After school, a few of the guys caught up to me while I was walking home and asked me if I was ok. I simply said yes and kept walking. They could see I wasn't myself, and finally the leader of the crew my age finally confronted me and pushed me. Out of fear, I started running but didn't make it that far. They caught up to me behind a gas station and gave me the worst beating of my life. Two older men finally came and got them off me. I was lucky because one of them knew my older brother, and he put me in his car and drove me home.

When I got home, my mother was in the front watering her plants. When she saw my face, and I told her what had happened, she went into a crazy panic, started cussing, and told my older brother to get the keys to the car. My mother has always been an intense protector. My brother and I were able to calm her down a bit. He said, "Mom, if you really want him to get away from them, you have to let this happen." My mother was confused and still very angry, but once one of my other brothers showed up, she listened. You see, this older brother was in that life. He had just turned 18 and was considered one of the most powerful youngsters in town. But even he couldn't stop this. He assured my mom that the worst was over and that I just had to deal with this until they got over it. It was called "jumping out." It's when you declare that you do not want to be part of that life anymore, and trust me, they don't let you off easy and sometimes not at all. I was lucky. They kicked the crap out of me after school for four straight days. The last day was not so bad. I still got my ass kicked, but by then I couldn't feel my face, so I fought back with all I had.

The entire school knew what happened. My mother never complained to the school, and when teachers asked me what happened, I told them what Daniel-san told Mr. Miyagi, "I fell off my bike." The crew made sure that all the students were warned. Anyone who hung around me was subject to the same treatment. So, as you can imagine, I was a loner for a long time.

Finally, three or four months later, a kid named James Kliegl asked me to throw the football around with him at recess. I mustered up the courage to get out there with him and his friends, and immediately we hit it off. He asked me to come over to his house sometime, and from that day forward we became very good friends. Later that week, I went over his house only to be confronted by his father at the door asking if I had done my homework already. I was in shock. I had never been asked if I did my homework by anyone, sometimes not even my teachers. Mr. Kliegl was a firm but caring man. To this day I admire him for how he and his wife Janet raised their children and how he welcomed me when everyone else judged and made sure their kids stayed away from me.

James was half Mexican but looked like Opie Taylor. Only two out of the dozen or so of his friends were Mexican, so that became another thing to hold against me. In most of the Mexican kid's eyes I was now "White-washed." The crazy thing is that a lot of the White kids would still call me wetback or greaser. I didn't care. I now had a friend who was pushing me to do my homework and enroll in sports and who didn't seem to mind that he was in danger doing so. My decision was made; this was me now. I would go on to qualify for advance classes when just one year earlier I couldn't read English. I was now the quarterback of our football team and an all-star baseball player. Even with identity issues, I was now alive! I eventually became very comfortable in my own skin regardless of what people said. It took me a few years, but I grew to believe in myself. That belief translated into athletics, and I also became very observant and started making entrepreneurial moves. Whether it was marbles, cinnamon paper, candy, or working in the fields, I always had a hustle going.

The two brothers who were the leaders of the crew I rolled with were convicted for murdering a man just three years later in a drug deal gone wrong. The younger brother was one of my best friends. I wonder where I would be if I hadn't made the choice to change my direction in life. I could have been there...that could have been me. My friend has since passed away and his brother served 20 years for murder. He has been out for a few years now, has married his childhood sweetheart, and has made a good life for himself.

I am blessed to have so many great people in my life. It is those people that have tremendously impacted my life with their love, support, and understanding. Surrounding myself with great people who are also ambitious and who are also focused on personal growth is probably the smartest decision I have ever made. What a blessing to have been confronted with life-defining moments and in them find my identity.

I now find myself enjoying a great life that, although it has its challenges, reminds me everyday of just how far I have come. I own a real estate company in Bakersfield, California, and I am in the middle of opening two other businesses and writing my first book. I have a beautiful wife and two kids that love and support my craziness. I am proud to say that God's grace and my choices got me here. These moments have given me the confidence that I know I will have to lean on as they continue to come and shape my life.

Life-defining moments have no time or age criteria. They are the moments that life throws at us where critical decisions must be made. We never have control of when they come or how they hit us. What we do have control over is how we respond to them. I don't claim to have always responded in ways that were productive or even positive. What I do know is that without important people in our lives, it is damned near impossible to make it through. God sends the right people at the right time, we just must pay attention.

I am grateful for my life and each of its defining moments. Tackle your life-defining moments with confidence and excitement because the more you are faced with them, the more you are alive! Now go live, live freely and live in the moment because the moment just might be life-defining.

TWEETABLE

What a blessing to have been confronted with life defining moments and in them find my identity.

Freddy Perez is an industry leader, owning the highest production per agent real estate company in California's Central Valley. Speaker, leader in personal development, high-level coach in Bakersfield.

His "Success Through Others" and "Mastering Your Mind" philosophies have made him one of the most sought-after speakers/presenters in the business.

freddy@freddyperez.net
Instagram: @freddyperezperformance
Facebook: Freddy Perez
www.freddyperez.net

CHAPTER 9

Slaying Your Giant

by Mark and Tamiel Kenney

Finding peace in a chaotic world can be challenging. It seems like our lives just keep getting busier and more complex as time goes on. Maybe it is our culture or our own individual choices that create this chaos, but having a plan to survive and thrive in the chaos is key to living a life well lived. In order to obtain the success in life we hope to achieve, there will always be challenges to tackle and giants to face. It is in these moments of trial that we discover who we are. It just might take slaying a few giants to reveal your purpose. Are you ready to take on your giant?

Our most recent obstacle felt like a giant. We hope that as you read our story, you will realize three things: You are stronger than you think; You can slay your giant no matter his size; With great trials come greater rewards, if you don't give up. We want you to know that you are not alone. Fight the good fight and always do what's right.

"The strong person is the one who knows how to be quiet, shed a tear for a moment, and then picks up their gloves and fights again!"

They said "you are playing with the big boys now" when our $15 million real estate deal was in jeopardy. We personally had $200,000 of our own money on the line for this deal that took us six months to find. Mark would have had to take an IT contract job to support our family had this deal fallen through. Our $5 million equity raise should have been easy, and it was, until suddenly it wasn't. We were terrified!

A week earlier, we were excited about the purchase of this apartment complex. It was our biggest purchase at the time, in a good area of Dallas. We were on target to raise all the money we needed within a few days, when all of a sudden, people who had committed to invest in the deal backed out. Several investors reached out to us right away to let us know why they chose not to invest in our apartment deal. Others remained silent but were no longer interested. Even several months later, a few more investors expressed their disappointment that they did not invest with us after they heard how great the deal was performing. The apartment community was purchased for $15.4M and after one year was now worth $23M...not too bad!

"Leadership is based on inspiration, not domination; on cooperation, not intimidation."

All of these investors admittedly chose not to invest with us because of a disagreement we had with our community organizer. It had nothing to do with the deal and nothing to do with us, rather it was due to a personality conflict between our partner and the community organizer. It's especially unfortunate when this happens with someone who you look up to, someone who is your mentor. We did not feel like we could take our mentor's advice in good conscience. To our dismay, this created a ripple within the community that made it much more difficult for us to accomplish our goals. We felt personally attacked by some of the stories that were circulating.

"Sometimes you wanna go, where everybody knows your name."

If you grew up in the 80s you may remember the theme song from Cheers. There is something to be said about being a part of a community. Good or bad, you still feel like you are a part of something. We had been a part of a real estate investor community for almost three years. We met many people that we really liked and a few that became really good friends.

But…sometimes things change. People change. Even long-term friendships can change. The Real Estate Guys™ have said that time will either promote you or expose you. We have found that to be true on more than one occasion. We see that money does not change people, it only exposes them.

Not only was our deal in jeopardy, our future deals were in jeopardy too. We now have investors that will not consider investing with us in the future out of fear of the situation. I like to say that we have enough stories to create our own reality TV show! There is currently a show called American Greed. It talks about the dark side of the American dream and shows how far some people go to become rich, no matter the cost to themselves and those around them. Even though we see it, we feel it, we are living it…I choose to have hope in the future and in people. It is my hope that every person has the strength to stand up for what they believe is right.

"You may see me struggle, but you will never see me quit."

I understand that it may feel like the easiest solution to conflict is to avoid it, especially when it appears you face a stronger foe. We have faced many of our own personal struggles, in business and even in our marriage, because we avoided conflict or communicated poorly about it. But I assure you, the only true way to make a problem go away is to deal with it!

"You can sweep all your problems under a rug, but sooner or later someone is gonna pick up the rug and shake it."

The truth about problems is that they don't just disappear. Sweeping our problems under the rug only takes them out of sight while they continue to grow over time. Eventually, problems will need to be faced. But what do you do when you are faced with an obstacle or problem that seems too big to overcome?

"The true warrior isn't immune to fear, she fights in spite of it."

When all you see is the problem, you stop working toward the solution. Stress can cloud your vision, if you allow it. It is not the stress that would limit us but our reaction to it. So, we had to make a choice. We chose to be victors and not victims. Once we changed our mindset, our vision for our future became clear. With much prayer and angst, we knew we had to form our own real estate education company. We were going to create our own community!

"And suddenly you know—It's time to start something new and trust the magic of new beginnings."

Starting a new chapter in life can be intimidating. But as every author knows, writing a good story must begin with the 5 W's: Who, What, Where, When, and Why. Once we were clear on what we were creating, for whom it was being created, and why we were starting something new, the real work began. Our fear continued, but our passion for what we were doing was greater! God had given us a clear vision for creating our new company, and we had to just step out in faith and begin the work. We worked 14-16 hour days for weeks, even months on end, to form what is now Think Multifamily, a multifamily acquisition and education company. We are a community of investors who share the same values of leading with integrity. We believe in helping others change their lives and their legacy through apartment investing. We understand that this is more than just a business to us, it is a family!

Become a Ninja

I don't watch much television, but I have to admit that I do like to watch American Ninja Warrior. This show is an action-packed series that follows competitors as they tackle a sequence of challenging obstacles. I love to hear the stories of personal and physical difficulties that some of these athletes have had to conquer to get themselves to this point of competition. You can see a pattern of overcoming struggles that has made these athletes stronger and given them the courage and confidence to continue to take down obstacles in life as well as in this show.

Slay the Giant

If you are familiar with Bible stories, the story of David and Goliath offers encouragement to many. Goliath was a giant who intimidated and threatened the Jewish army. As soldiers, you would think they were trained to be fearless, but that was not the case. Not one of those soldiers, including the king himself, was courageous enough to face that giant. They were merely men, who were faced with the same fight or flight response to fearful or stressful situations that we face today.

The fight or flight response is our body's natural, instinctive way to respond to stress as a means of self-preservation. However, a habit or pattern of negative response to stress based on past experiences, can be termed "learned helplessness." According to an article in The Huffington Post, "If left unchecked, this pattern of 'learned' avoidant behaviors will lead to passive and poor decisions."

To continue this story, a young man named David had heard about Goliath and yet he was not afraid. He agreed to fight this giant, without the protection of armor offered by the king and without the support of his brothers in the army, who were all too afraid to fight. But God had put a fire in David. He had faith, in spite of the fear. Fear can overwhelm us, but sometimes all you have to do is change your perspective to see the light.

"Sometimes God will put a Goliath in your path, for you to find the 'David' in you."

How did young David have such courage to fight this battle? Because over time, and with repeated success over previous battles, David had built up the faith and courage to face the next obstacle or giant that came his way. David slayed Goliath that day, as he freed the Jewish people from the fear and intimidation of death and slavery that would have followed had he lost.

"Your circumstances do not define you. Expect a grand finale!"

Shift Your Perspective

Difficult situations are inevitable. But praise God, problems are only for a season. When we are able to take a step back and see the situation from a different perspective, then, clarity comes. Problems are simply obstacles that can be overcome, one at a time. Like the American Ninja Warrior, who must conquer one obstacle and then another, to take them closer to their ultimate goal of ringing that bell at the end of the course; you too can conquer your obstacle one step and one day at a time.

So, what do you do when your problem is in an extended season and the stress has really begun to build? What do you do when your obstacles seem bigger than you are capable of conquering alone?

"Life isn't about waiting for a storm to pass. It is about learning to dance in the rain."

Find Peace

Even when we understand problems are only for a season, sometimes our emotions can still get the best of us. When a particularly difficult season seems to drag on and on with no end in sight, stress does tend to build, which takes a toll on us, physically, mentally, emotionally, and spiritually. Or when the problem seems too big for us to face alone, we feel overwhelmed and don't know which direction to turn.

Finding our own inner peace in the midst of these trials is key to our success. We can have joy even though our situation is difficult. We can learn to see these challenges as something to make us stronger, better, wiser. Believing that something "awesome" is waiting for you on the other side of the wall can give you the peace, joy, and mental clarity that has been hiding just out of sight.

Release the Stress

Stress is inevitable for each of us, but it is always good to learn ways that can help to minimize it.

Here are a few suggestions to minimize stress:

a. Start your day in prayer or meditation, if only for 5-10 minutes.

b. Take a walk or do some physical activity to release mood elevating endorphins.

c. Keep a journal of your thoughts and perhaps any insights or lessons learned.

d. Create a thankful jar. Write on a notecard everything you are thankful for and place it in a jar. When you need that extra boost of encouragement, pull out the cards and read them out loud.

e. Create a vision board to establish personal goals.

f. Take your mind off of your current situation and focus on your future.

Make a Choice

Ultimately you get to choose who you will become in this process. Will you choose fear or will you choose joy? Will you choose passivity or will you choose to be the ninja warrior I know is inside of you? We have the power to choose: life or death, fear or joy, fight or flight, hide or seek, victim or victor. We get to choose to be FREE or held captive by our fear, our failure, or our situation.

Because of the obstacles in my own life, I am growing stronger, becoming more courageous, and building my faith. Make declarative statements about yourself today that will help define who you choose to be and how you choose to live.

Here are my declarative statements:

I choose to fight,
I will not cower

I choose to lead,
And not blindly follow

I choose joy,
And not fear

I will speak up for what is right,
And not be silenced by intimidation

I will lead with integrity,
And not give in to the easy road

I am a warrior and so are you! I have finally found the David in me. I hope that you will find the David in you too!

TWEETABLE

Choose to be a victor and not a victim. Change your mindset, and the vision for your future becomes clear.

Mark and Tamiel Kenney are #1 Amazon Best Selling Authors, parents of two, and founders of Think Multifamily, a Multifamily Real Estate Investing Acquisition, Education & Mentoring company. Connect with them on social media or at tami@thinkmultifamily.com.

CHAPTER 10

Run Your Own Race, Advice from an Emmy-Winning Sportscaster

by Newy Scruggs

want people to know they've got to run their own race. Your race.

A military base is very different than the civilian world. It just is. My dad was in the military and my family moved around a lot. I lived a lot of different places with a whole lot of different people. I could be at a school where I was only one of maybe five Black kids in the class or I could be at a school where there were only five White kids in a class. One of the things I started to learn as I got older is that people try to put folks in boxes.

My dad grew up in segregated Birmingham, Alabama, when it was known as Bombingham. It was THE worst city to be Black in America. My dad was sprayed by the ultra-segregationist City of Birmingham's City Commissioner of Public Safety Bull Connor's hoses for demanding equal treatment. In 1963, when Martin Luther King was in the Birmingham jail, my dad, who was just 17 at the time, was in the same jail with him. They used kids for those demonstrations. The parents had to go to work. Black people couldn't take the day to go demonstrate; in the South you would get fired, so MLK used kids.

Look, my dad was strict. In the military there's a standard. You go to school and you get good grades. That was our job as kids.

I find it disturbing today; for many young Black youth, if you're seen doing the schoolwork and you're seen as smart, people will make fun of you. Nobody wants to be seen as another Steve Urkel, the nerdy black kid in the TV sitcom *Family Matters*. I experienced the questions and snide insults for being a student who did well in school through college: "Whatchu doing?", "We all can't be smart brother" and my favorite zinger, "You sound white." The frustrating part of those put-downs was, I wasn't the smartest guy around. I was surrounded by better Black male students, but in our formative years we tend to feel as though we are the only person being singled out.

I have always liked music. Even though I'm a Texan now, I don't like country music. Hate it, except for old school Kenny Rogers tunes and one Darius Rucker tune, "Don't Think I Don't Think About It." Outside of country, I like a lot of different music. Growing up in the 80s, everybody loved Hall & Oates. "Man Eater" is a great song! Who doesn't like that song? I mainly listened to rap and R&B but for some reason friends and teammates wanted to understand my other taste for groups like The Police, Chicago, and Van Halen. "Why are you listening to that White boy music for?" My best buds on the football team almost made me feel that I could only listen to RUN-DMC, Big Daddy Kane, Public Enemy, or Guy, which I did, but I never limited myself.

The importance of running your own race showed up for me less than ten years later. I was living and working in Los Angeles, and I remember being at one of the hottest spots in town, the Century Club, on a Sunday night. The floor was packed and people were jamming to the number hit "I'll Be Missing You" by Puff Daddy. The rap tune heavily samples the song "Every Breath You Take" by wait for it...The Police! That song would win a Grammy Award for Best Rap Performance for a duo or group. See, I wasn't crazy.

Good music is good music. Later in my own quest for self education I learned that Black musicians in the Deep South were the main influences that created rock and roll. Robert Johnson, Muddy Waters, Fats Domino, Little Richard inspired great performers like Elvis, The Beatles, and the Rolling Stones. The Beatles wanted Little Richard to be their manager. The Rolling Stones named their group after a Muddy Waters song. I love the rapper Ice-T's lines when he responded to critics who didn't understand why he, as a respected hip hop artist, also fronted his heavy metal band Body Count. He said, "I never ran with a lotta [dudes]. I only ran with the real [dudes], you know what I'm saying? And if you ain't willing to do [it] your way, then you have to copy a lotta [dudes] and a copy can't be real, it can only be counterfeit, and alotta [dudes] will never figure that [one] out."

I knew I wanted to be a TV sportscaster since 5th grade. I was 11 years old. In Mr. McDuffie's class in Savannah, Georgia, we a did a mock newscast. I absolutely loved it. It was fun. That's when I knew what I wanted to do. But there's a difference between kind of knowing and hoping and actually doing and going through the action steps to get yourself there.

When I was 17 years old in high school in North Carolina I finally figured out that I had to run my own race, and I was able to put my action plan to use.

I was in Mr. Stanton's class at Westover Senior High School. Nobody keeps notes from an English class they took as a junior in high school, but I have.

I've got this brown binder. I read the works of Emerson and Thoreau. I was inspired by Henry David Thoreau writing that you should follow your genius closely enough and it will never fail you. He wrote in Walden, "By my experiment: that if one advances confidently in the direction of his dreams, and endeavors to live the life which he has imagined, he will meet with a success unexpected in common hours."

Ralph Waldo Emerson was dropping what would be major motivational nuggets for me in his The Essay on Self-Reliance. His rule of greatness was so epic to me because he really was simple when he conveyed, "What I must do is all that concerns me, not what the people think."

Boom! Mic drop! Game over! I was on my way because, at 17, Emerson was saying to me to just run my own race and forget the voices, the peer pressure, and the expectations of others. I was a changed and clearheaded individual after soaking in that education.

Later that year in high school I read a book that was also life-defining, *Showtime: Inside the Lakers' Breakthrough Season* by Lakers coach Pat Riley. It really solidified what I had been catching on to. On a side note, Pat Riley got around some smart marketers like Kyle Wilson, because he ended up making a bunch of money by writing a book with the same principles from *Showtime*, but for business, titled *The Winner Within: A Life Plan For Team Players*.

What I learned in that book, which changed so many things around me, is that you have to know who you are. As Pat famously quotes his dad, "Every now and then, somewhere, someplace, sometime, you are going to have to plant your feet, make a stand firm, and kick some ass. And when that time comes, you do it."

The lesson in that quote nugget for me was how you have to believe and fight for your dreams and goals. Who are you going to be? What are you going to be? And what are you chasing?

I figured out at 17 years old, I didn't have to please everybody. I didn't have to please the friends around me. I had this dream about being a sportscaster. That's all I needed to work on, my dream.

Pat Riley's best chapter in *Showtime* is called Motivation. Chapter 13. I still have the beat up paperback copy published in 1988 with yellow highlighter marking his words on how he stays motivated, "...when you can put those two things together, what you need and what you want—there's your motivation. Keep that situation alive. Be so good at it that they can't even think about replacing you."

I reread Chapter 13 often, every other month at least. It's only two pages. I read it and think, "Oh my gosh, no wonder this man was so good as a coach, winning five NBA titles with the Lakers and Miami Heat and ultimately reaching the ultimate honor of his sport, induction into the Basketball Hall of Fame." That book helped me define what I wanted for my life.

You had to have self-confidence to not let other people's doubts get to you. My dad didn't want me to do this. My dad wanted me to be a lawyer. He grew up in Birmingham. Black folks were rarely on TV news even when I was a kid. When they were put on TV, they were light-skinned like Bryant Gumble. I'm not light-skinned. When networks put Black people on TV news they were in shape and cute. I'm not. I'm porky and chunky all day long. So, my dad discouraged me. You don't want your kids to chase some dream. You want your kids to do something that's more secure.

Honestly, I was too stupid to expect anything but success, too stupid to know what I didn't know. I would not recommend trying to do this. I would not. I mean, there's only four sports television jobs like I have here in Dallas, the fifth largest TV market in the nation. I'm glad I didn't know how hard it was going to be, how improbable it would be for me to succeed!

At another high school in town, the top sports anchor in Raleigh, Tom Suiter, was giving a speech to the student government group in February of 1987. I loved Tom. I used to watch him every night on WRAL's six o'clock news and Football Friday at 11:30 at night. I went and met him. He was kind, and we developed a relationship. We became pen pals. Eventually he let me come up to the television station, and I was able to tap into him for knowledge about becoming a sportscaster. My dream was to attend the University of North Carolina. That was the best broadcast journalism school in the state, and I was a major Tar Heels basketball fan. I still am today. But Tommy told me that Carolina might not be the best choice. He said, "They don't touch anything there; they don't DO anything. Go someplace where you can get hands-on experience." I never applied to Carolina.

God works in mysterious ways. In the local paper, *The Fayetteville Observer*, two weeks later there was a big spread about Pembroke State University's television program WPSU. The article told of how the Pembroke State students did everything. They ran everything in the program. That was the experience Tom Suiter was talking about. This small regional college in Southeastern North Carolina was the place I needed to go to learn the craft. I got a scholarship to go to Pembroke State.

I wish I could say people didn't question my decision. Those around me said a degree from Carolina would open more doors for me. It had a reputation for producing journalists. Pembroke State did not. Without the lessons of

Thoreau and the book Showtime, maybe I would have listened to them. Instead, I had the confidence in me to listen to my mentor. What I needed to do was get experience.

Sure enough, my freshman year I was working at WPSU-TV. I even served as a TV color commentator for two basketball games for the PSU Braves. I was attacking this television program and sportscasting the way a basketball player or tennis player works on their game. I was in it every day, all the time doing it. The professor who recruited me told me though, "You need to not just think about sports. You're not going to get a job in TV sports when you leave here." So I was the guy looking out for internships, trying to figure out where can I go, how can I get more experience. I made my own business cards. I was constantly asking what can I do to get my foot in the door. I talked to as many people as possible because I wanted to do this. And he was right; I didn't get a job in TV or sports when I left school. I got that job before I left!

I sacrificed to work full-time at CBS in Florence/Myrtle Beach, South Carolina, while going to college full-time my senior year. I was not a guy who went out and partied. As a weekend sports anchor and reporter you can kiss a social life goodbye. The schedule means you work nights on Fridays, Saturdays, and Sundays. Holidays were just regular days for new folks in the business.

Time flies. It wasn't long before I realized that I had achieved more success than I had ever dreamed of. I had worked my way up from South Carolina, to Austin, Texas, Cleveland, and then Los Angeles as an award-winning weekday lead sports anchor. These days I am the sports director at KXAS-TV (NBC) in Dallas-Ft. Worth with seven Emmys under my belt.

One thing that my mom and dad always told me is, we want you to take care of yourself. I know I've made my parents proud. My success I can attribute to the work ethic and standards they raised me with and that ability to run my own race.

I have a very strong work ethic, but when you're around military people the way I was—they were high achievers. My dad was in the First Cavalry, the 82nd Airborne and an Army Ranger. That's the creme de la creme. In my family I'M the lazy one. My work ethic has nothing on my parents. I wasn't making a lot of money. There are a lot of people who start out in television who quit because in television news you start out in low TV market cities like a minor league baseball player. If you want to live this dream you are tested early on. My work ethic helped me keep going.

I succeeded because of my willingness to work—all the time. I work in the job of inconvenience. You just can't plan it; things just happen and you have to figure it out. My wife had our second child July 25, 2006 and six days later I was at the Dallas Cowboys training camp in Oxnard. It was the controversial Terrell Owen's first year and my boss wanted all the coverage we could get. So I left my wife with my mom with two kids aged 22 months apart. I am lucky that I have a partner who understands that this is the job.

I showed up. I showed up. And I showed up on days I didn't have to show up. My off day was a work day for me. My off day was still a day I needed to go out places and talk to people and be seen. Ultimately, after a while you start to get to know more and more people. You build up your Rolodex of contacts and then you have opportunities to tell good stories and have inside information. You'd be surprised how many people don't want to work hard in my industry. The trend today I find is a lot people just want to "be on TV." They want the perceived celebrity of the job.

You need to work hard, and you need to have confidence in yourself. I knew what I wanted to do. And I don't live my life trying to make sure other people are agreeing with me or letting other people tell me what is good. You'd be surprised how many people are insecure in my business, how many pep talks I constantly have to give people, people you've seen on TV.

I'm proof Thoreau was right. I put in the time to advance confidently in the direction of my dreams, and I have lived the life I imagined. From covering Super Bowls, NBA Finals, college football playoff games, World Series, championship boxing matches, and men's and women's final fours. I have lived the dream.

I had the vision that this is what I want to do. I listened to the things that I like, and I still do to this day. I'm not going to let anyone else define me and put me in these boxes. As Steve Martin says, "Be so good they can't ignore you."

Thank goodness I ran my own race. I hope you do the same.

My next race is building my own public speaking and coaching business.

TWEETABLE

What I must do is all that concerns me, not what the others may think — Emerson's Rule of Greatness

Seven-time Emmy-winner Newy Scruggs is the sports director at KXAS-TV (NBC) in Dallas-Ft. Worth, Texas. You can catch him weeknights at 6 and 10. Sundays, during the NFL season, Scruggs hosts the Emmy Award winning Out of Bounds *with Dallas Cowboys Ring of Honor member Drew Pearson.*

Scruggs has been in broadcasting since 1992. Along the way the stops have included gigs in Florence/ Myrtle Beach, South Carolina; Austin, Texas; Cleveland; Los Angeles; and since April 2000 in Dallas-Fort Worth.

Twitter: @newyscruggs
Facebook: NewyScruggsSports
www.newdawg.com

CHAPTER 11

What If What Looks Like a Curse is Your Life's Biggest Blessing?

by Ravin Souvendra Papiah

"He is going to die an early death—he is too weak to sustain. I give him a maximum of ten years." said the doctor to my mother.

That's exactly 52 years back!

I was born a very weak child in Mauritius, a small island country west of India. My parents and older brothers and sisters told me that I stayed in the hospital for quite a long time compared to the normal newborns.

But thank God, my mother didn't believe the doctor. She cared for me constantly and extremely well, taking me to the best doctors despite our very severe and distressful financial situation. I practically lived on drugs and injections all throughout my childhood.

When I was ready to go to pre-primary school, my mother sent my eldest sister with me. She stayed the whole day with me at school, everyday. She cared for me same like a mother. I felt secured.

Because of my sick nature, I was not allowed to go out and play with other kids. Because socialization was not there at school, I was afraid to go to school alone. My sister, now my second mother, was my entire security. I loved school—I love the scent of the writing slate and the pencil. I loved scribing. I loved painting and playing with colors. But I didn't like to stay alone at school.

Primary school came, and now I had to stay at school the whole day alone. My sister was not allowed to stay in the class with me. That rendered me sicker, and every two or three days, during the morning prayer session, I would fall unconscious. The other students will shout "Sir! Madam! The boy fell unconscious again!" That happened two to three times a week. At a time when the phone was a luxury, the news was conveyed to my house, half a kilometer away from school, by an attendant. My parents and elder siblings being at work, my 65-year-old landlord would come to fetch me from the school. I can still hear his heavy breathing while carrying me up the hill to my home. I will never forget him and his noble actions towards me so many times. I will forever be grateful.

I never played at school—I was not authorized to go and play outside during the recreation period. My teacher (Miss Chantal) would sit in the class and watch over me. She would look at me, and I would look at her, pondering what we could have done to deserve such a punishment. It was more so for my teacher, whose colleagues were having great moments during the break, cracking jokes and having fun among other colleague teachers, while she was having to watch on me!

One day, my teacher called me to her desk while we were having our daily "break" meeting. She asked me, "Would you like to read?" I was barely six years old and could not really understand her question. I looked at her with inquiring and bewildered eyes, partly petrified, partly curious. I just shook my head in a positive manner.

She said, "Bring your chair here."

I took my chair and approached her. She made me sit very near to her. I was quite uncomfortable and wanted just to run away. She put her hand on my shoulder and said, "You're a good boy, now you are going to become a good reader as well!" She had a big smile on her face. I got a bit relaxed. And she started imparting to me the skill of reading.

She read slowly to me, making sure I could hear her and understand every word she was uttering. She read, word by word, then made me spell and repeat the word, telling me what it meant and asking me to repeat the spelling after her. I read lines and lines during all the days we were together, all the year round.

At seven years of age, I was reading books like Enid Blyton's The Famous Five and The Secret Seven. I read the entire collection available then, a rare feat for a child of my age at that time! When every other child of my class was playing, I was learning to read and reading progressively by myself. I enjoyed the journey, and kept spending all my spare time reading books. I was reading between 7 and 10 books every week, renting them from the school's library or village council free libraries. Books changed my life. I was seeing and living my dreams in the stories of characters featured in the books. I was relishing my "virtual" world and kept myself lost there for hours in my spare and free time. I even attended my nature calls bringing a book with me!

I was a very introverted and timid child. I was afraid of meeting and talking to people. When guests or relatives came home, I would hide in my room, sometimes under the bed! I was kind of anti-social, not really, but never getting the opportunity to socialize with my school friends made me like that. I didn't socialize, first, because of the ban on my playing outside because of my medical condition and, second, because the other children were always laughing at me and bullying me because of the way I was, so I stayed away.

But like every other child, I also wanted to have friends. I wanted to play. I wanted to do all these little things that children could do while on recreation time. Eating all kinds of sweets and snacks—I was not allowed to do so. Thus, I took my comfort in my books. I found my friends in my books. I found my role in my books. Whatever I could not do or be in real life, I was being and doing in the books. I was the hero of the stories, and I played the character in my mind while I was reading, producing my own "virtual" film. I was content.

But with time, and while growing into a teen, I started reading bigger books, more serious books of fiction, like the book *Sandokan*, and also several cartoons like *Tintin*, *Zembla*, *Akim*, *Blek le Roc*, *Mustang*, *Kiwi* and many others. These stories infused many things in me, like the desire to be a hero, to be strong and muscular, to be fighting for what is right, to be winning over enemies, and most importantly to be able to speak to others— as simple as that.

My love and obsession for books never stopped. I had a gargantuan appetite for reading. And this is something I continued to nurture and cultivate during all the years of my life.

Through books, through the various stories, I got inspired to BECOME more than what I was. The burning desire to become more reflected in my school results. I was always first in every subject at school, despite my big handicap of consistent sickness that pulled me out of school nearly half of the time I should have been there. But I still managed to come out first, every time. At the end of my primary schooling, I earned my school, The Swami Sivananda Government School at Tyack, Mauritius, its first ever scholarship winner—ME! At the young age of 10 years, I was competing with kids years older than me!

That got me a seat at a five-star state college, but because of my medical condition, my parents opted to send me to a normal government college nearer to home. But, that was not a reason not to do well there. I passed the school certificate with the best results in my village, completed my higher school certificate with great results, and got a job at 19 years old as a bank officer.

I stayed at the bank for about seven years. After three years, having got married and awaiting the coming of my first child, a son, I took on a part-time job in direct selling to add to my income. This was very difficult for me as I was a shy guy, and I had to go from door to door, giving presentations and cooking live to demonstrate the quality of the products. I got solace in the fact that this would solve my financial problems, and I could give to my child whatever he deserved to have a great childhood. So, I went forward, doing it afraid and taking the heroes of my books as my inspiration and my models.

This was a wonderful experience that offered me a platform to grow myself, allowed me to conquer my fear of speaking, and helped me to connect with more people, thus making me become more confident in myself. With more confidence, I saw my competence in communication and selling soaring, and I was able to have four years of excellent part-time income that created a better life for my family, helping me manage to take a mortgage to build my own house at the young age of 26.

At that particular time, my part-time company introduced a new product on the market—a set of encyclopedias and other sets of books for students of all ages—and I started selling that too. I did extremely well in the first months, and they offered me a full time opportunity as a freelance branch manager for those products. I left the bank to take on that job in spite of all my family members' discontentment. I was given a guaranteed salary four times my bank salary at the time of my resignation there, to ensure the first year went on smoothly for me. But I never needed that minimum guaranteed salary. In the first month I made seven times my salary at the bank, and I continued to grow in that job.

While my personal growth was taking flight, I did not have any management training in the selling and salesforce management. SO I made a lot of mistakes due to ignorance. I used the Pareto principle of 80/20 in reverse. I was using my hard-earned money to motivate my team members, but I was giving away too much and keeping very little for me. That brought chaos several years later. Despite winning eight consecutive international championships for my results in the eight years, I made no money, and moreover, I contracted some overdrafts to keep managing and motivating my team. I gave away too much, and that brought my dream to shatter in 1998. I lost everything: my house, my marriage, my career. Everything was gone in dust!

Fortunately, my thirst for reading brought me to discover the world of personal development in the late 90s. My very good friend from South Africa, Val Leech, introduced me to Jim Rohn. I started by subscribing to Jim's free e-zine and eventually grew to own all of his available products.

These products completely changed my life at a time when I was undergoing one of the most painful moments of my life. I lost my job, went through a divorce and was alone without any resources of any kind with my two kids of seven and eight years old. But that was also my win! My kids, the most prized of my assets, were with me.

It took me about 14 years to recover from that situation, but God blessed me with the wisdom of Jim Rohn and several other mentors whom I've known through Jim during my journey in the desert. My appetite for reading, and researching, and discovering helped me find new ways, new solutions, and new creativity to build a new life for me and my family.

From 1998 to 2017, I have experienced the lowest of the lows and the highest of the highs. I believe I was able to navigate through the worst of situations to ultimately find myself at higher levels of achievement and success every time, thank to the consistent upliftment from my children and my life partner, Rageeni, my mentors, and the lessons I got from books. Today, I am the CEO in two of my companies, and I work with one of the best, if not the best, network marketing company in the world. I am out of financial distress, not yet financially independent, but getting there slowly but surely.

My quest for more and my thirst for personal growth eventually landed me an opportunity to become a Founding Member and a Certified Trainer of the John Maxwell Team and with Gitomer Licensed Trainers. I have had the opportunity to be coached by Jim Rohn's 18-year business partner and marketing genius, the great Kyle Wilson, with whom and many other great collaborators, I am contributing to this book.

I am today training at the corporate level to share my story, my journey from rags to riches, and my consistent fight to eventually live the life I have always wanted. It is a story of tenacity, resilience, patience, belief, and faith. And I believe it all sprouted from the fact that I was coached to read at a very young age due to my adversity at that time. It is very right to say then that the fact that I was not allowed to go out and play with my friends during the recreation was a defining moment for me, which in fact gave me an opportunity to become the person I am today, a person I would have never believed I could become years ago!

For this, I can only thank my teacher, Miss Chantal, for introducing me to the feat of reading at such an early age and transforming my vulnerability into a force. Because of this, today I am able to contribute to this book, which I hope will show many other "Ravin" in this world a way to build their best version of themselves and thus live a better life and enhance the lives of others through humility and sharing their experience with the world.

TWEETABLE

Mine is a story of tenacity, resilience, patience, belief, and faith sprouted from the fact that I was coached to read at a very young age.

Ravin S. Papiah is passionate about helping others reach their highest potential. Currently a founder partner and a certified coach, speaker & trainer, and an executive director of the John Maxwell Team, a Gitomer Licensed Trainer, managing director of the Mighty Champs Marketing Co. Ltd. and the Professional Leadership Centre Ltd, and previously president of Plateau Toastmasters Club, Mauritius, Ravin is highly decorated in the industries of professional speaking and direct selling.

www.johncmaxwellgroup.comravinsouvendrapapiah/About

CHAPTER 12

Me, Myself & The Supershero

by Amada Chan

I recently folded a startup business that I "experimented" with for over two years. Although the experiment was successful, the business failed. After two years of experimentation, I sat down and had a conversation with myself to evaluate my business report card.

I sat in my office staring at the startup business logo that I designed, pinned on a plain empty wall. I used to do that to inspire myself, but this time my brain was as plain and empty as the wall. The inspirations died and the only thing left was pieces of sadness. Then I heard…

"Hey, I hate to be so blunt, but it doesn't look like you made it to the Dean's List in this startup thing. What happened?" As I hear the words I see myself appear, in every way me except that she is not me. I talk to myself half jokingly, to break the ice.

"It's a BIG F. A lot of things happened, but yet, a lot didn't. I can't pinpoint one reason why we failed; instead there are many elements that didn't work together like the team, the model, and the market. It's just a BIG effing F." I answered.

"Any regrets?" I asked.

"No, no regret. Now that I gave it a try, I never have to wonder 'what if.' But after burying myself in the business for more than two years… (deep breath and sigh) and not getting the results that I wanted, I am exhausted and feel like I am a total loser. Our team built a product, people came, but they didn't stay. We couldn't figure it out. It was a black hole, sucking in all the time, effort, and money, and at the end, everything vanished into the dark." I replied with great disappointment.

"WOW, that sucks!" I said, feeling sorry for myself.

"It does. It totally sucked. I totally sucked at this." I shook my head.

Sinking my head down, I whispered "Ohh… I don't mean to say…. Hey, but at least you still have your real estate investment business to fall back on." purely attempting to deflect the focus.

"Haha…" with a sarcastic laugh, "What about it?"

"For most people, if their business failed, their life would turn upside down and the only thing that would come in the mail are delinquent payment notices, not rent checks. Bankruptcy and foreclosure is not uncommon. The next thing you know, they need to press life's 'Reset' button and start it all over again. You are far from that position. Your real estate business is still running on autopilot. In fact, the foundation of your real estate business is so strong, it allowed you to fund this experimental business venture for years. That's so freaking awesome!" I emphasized.

"So what?! My real estate is just real estate…It is doing what it is supposed to do because that's how I designed it. Real estate is easy." I said casually.

"Did you say 'real estate is easy?'" I was dumbfounded.

"Well, what I mean is, real estate is really not that complicated, and it's easy to figure it out. Plus the more you do, the easier it gets. The point is, I am not the sharpest knife in the drawer. If I can figure out real estate, anybody can. Trust me it is really no big deal!" I confirm my mediocrity with certainty. "And why are we talking about real estate, I thought we are doing an evaluation on the startup business report card!" I yelled out with frustration.

"Forget about the startup thing. You sucked at it anyway…. Sorry for being so honest! But listen to yourself. Real estate may be easy…for you, but it's not necessarily easy for anyone. Just like startups may be easy for some but not for you. It may be true that anyone can learn, but it doesn't mean anyone could be good at it. It's a big deal because apparently real estate is your talent, like Superman with superpowers. It's something that came naturally for you to learn, understand, and thrive on. If it is easy for you, it's in your DNA; therefore it is perceived to be "easy" according to you. Think about how many people you know lose money or even lose their livelihoods because of real estate. Do we need to go through the list to count how many real estate losers you know?! These people are all talented and have their superpower for something special, but real estate is their kryptonite. Do you see my point here?"

"Yeah yeah yeah, I see your point." I confirmed impatiently.

"Just look back at the last crash in 2008, your friends Bob and Tracey owned 15 investment properties but none of them cashflowed and they ended up filing for bankruptcy. Your other friend Allan lost three quarters of a million dollars investing in real estate that he knew nothing about. Those house flippers that you know all flopped. They were making a killing flipping houses and lost everything at the end. Also remember that guy Ryan, supposedly the "real estate guru" who sells books and podcasts "teaching" other people to invest. The guru himself also lost his fortune because he didn't even see the crash coming. The list goes on and on. So let me ask you, during the crash in 2008, what did you lose?"

I thought for a second and answered back slowly, "I didn't lose anything. Not a dime. I sold some of our properties for top dollar in 2006 and 2007 then sat on the sidelines and waited. A year later, the subprime mortgage storm arrived. It was surreal, and I was in disbelief. After the dust settled, I started shopping again because every block was on fire sale! And it didn't take me that long to build a solid portfolio to produce the income that I need. I mean, it wasn't overnight success, and it wasn't easy at the beginning. It was a steep learning curve, and it required a lot of hard work. The problem is most real estate investors are flippers, not keepers. Flippers focus on short-term gain. Keepers focus on long-term prosperity. True real estate investors are keepers. We have visions, and we have plans.

Real estate is not rocket science. It only requires 5th grade mathematics, but it needs a PhD in common sense. Contrary to popular beliefs, the notion of investing should be simple, logical, and most importantly, make common sense. If it cannot be explained in a tweet, it's too complicated. But, all too often, investors were sold the idea that investing is complicated and highly technical; therefore, they believe it must be. The truth is there are only a few key ingredients to a successful real estate investment, anything else is an add-on. That's why I said real estate is so easy..."

At that moment, a bolt of lightning struck me. My body was paralyzed and my brain was fried. I glanced around and found I was all alone. My imaginary self had left the room.

Suddenly a movie was playing inside my head in fast forward mode. It's a movie of my own real estate investing path beginning a decade ago. The opening scene started after I pressed my own life's "reset button" after being laid off. I was hopeless and helpless. I was at financial ground zero and working multiple odd jobs to get through the week because the entire month seemed too much and too long to bear. The word "investing" was not part of my vocabulary simply because I had no means to do so. Oddly, by some twist of fate, I ended up being in a real estate agent licensing class intending to become a real estate agent to make a living. Instead of becoming an agent, I learned a simple formula to kickstart my first real estate investment deal and launched my investing career. The journey was rocky, yet adventurous. Every chapter has its own peaks and valleys. Every deal comes with its own obstacle course, every turn has its bumps and hurdles, and every day is full of surprises, usually the unpleasant ones.

Now looking back, real estate is NOT that easy, much like anything in life is not easy. Anything worth pursuing is not meant to be easy. But after devoting more than a decade of my life to real estate investing, it does become easier.

For years, I took my own self for granted. I denied my own superpower, and I was too afraid to accept my greatness. I never allowed myself to admit I could do something amazing. I never dared to dream I could be somebody who could make a difference. Most of us are not trained to see beyond our own skin to discover our own abilities and develop our unique capabilities. Most of us are conditioned to believe success was reserved for a few mythical upper beings but never people like us.

Next time when you stand in front of the mirror, instead of searching for the blemishes on your face or the flaws on your body, meet the superhero in that reflection. You will be surprised how much you two have in common. Much like any new friendship, you may be intimidated and reserved at first, but don't hesitate to invite them to join your life venture together because with you, yourself, and the superhero, three is better than one.

TWEETABLE
Denying your own Superpower is your Kryptonite. Look in the mirror and see your Superhero self!

Amada Chan, Real Estate Entrepreneur, Techie, Designer

Amada, herself and the Supershero are currently working together as one on various real estate projects including acquisition, development, and real estate private equity funds to help others grow their wealth.

www.AmadaChan.com

CHAPTER 13

How Resistance Defined My Success

by Ron Jones

"Kites rise highest against the wind, not with it."

– Winston S. Churchill

I t has once been said that a kite flies to its highest point with resistance to the wind. I can honestly say that every major life-changing event in my life of true success came with resistance and challenges.

As I sat in a Sunday school classroom in a circle with six or seven other nine year olds, I hear the Sunday school teacher say that we are going to go around the room and read a couple of verses from the Bible. When I heard those words my heart started pounding with anxiety, I wasn't sure how I was going to get out of this because I didn't know how to read! What am I going to do? As time gets closer and closer to having to explain, I start to feel nauseated. When it is my turn, I passively tell the teacher that I don't want to read, without any explanation. That worked. I made it through again without being exposed as the Sunday school teacher told the next person to read the next set of verses without questioning me.

My mother at the age of 26 married my stepdad. We moved to Texas, and I was in the fourth grade. It was hard for me to understand at nine years old why I was being put back into the third grade, regardless of the fact that I did not know my ABCs and could not read. That's right, I could not read, and to this day I find it difficult to read out loud. I have long since released myself of the embarrassment I once had, but I know it is painful for others to listen to me in awkward silence, so I go out of my way to insure that I don't have to read out loud in front of others. From an early age I have learned to maneuver my way out of these situations. The challenge of dyslexia has made me be a better listener and has helped me work the part of the brain to memorize things that non-dyslexic people very likely take for granted.

I learned very early in life that I was not going to become a brain surgeon or rocket scientist, however I have never ever believed that I would not be successful. From the time I can remember, I have had an entrepreneurial spirit—shining shoes, delivering the town newspaper, and rummaging for Coke bottles to deposit so I could have lunch money.

By the time I was in high school I had become a master at maneuvering my way out of situations around reading out loud. In 1975 I was a sophomore and decided I would inquire as to how I could graduate with my class of 1976. After speaking with a school counselor, she and I mapped out a plan of my taking morning classes, Distributive Education (a school work program) allowing me to get class credit for working a job at McDonald's and a correspondence course from a local university. With a little hard work, and a girlfriend doing the correspondence course for me, I skipped my junior year and graduated from high school on the lower end the bell curve. You are very welcome, middle and upper classman of 1976!

Knowing that college was not an option for me at this point in my life, I decided the United States Air Force was going to be my best course of action. In June of 1976 I went to basic training. In basic training it didn't take long for my learning disability to come to the surface. I was an exceptional marksman and the fastest runner in my quad, but taking tests on what we were being taught in the classroom put me in the TIs office with him questioning my cognitive abilities. After convincing him that I could do it if he would just give me another opportunity, I recruited a twenty six year old in my squad to help me. I thank God for his patience and desire to help me to pass the test the second go around. To this day, I am not sure if I passed the test or if the TI saw that I really wanted to be there and took pity on me.

Tech school after boot camp created yet another set of challenges that I had to overcome. My saving grace in tech school was that I was given all the time I needed to take the multiple-choice and written test, and I excelled on the dexterity portion, which was the most important part of being a dental lab technician. I finished my service in the Air Force and was in the Texas Air National Guard for several years, all along hiding the fact that my reading skills were at approximately a 3rd grade level.

By the time I was twenty-four, my deep-seated entrepreneurial spirit had taken over and I started, owned, and operated three dental labs with 12 employees. After a couple of years, I ventured into real estate investments, mortgage banking, and construction to become a millionaire before the age of 27. With that being said, a kite does fly to its highest point with resistance to the wind. But common sense also would suggest that the kite will fall to the ground at some point. And the higher the kite flies, the harder it will fall to the ground, and that is what happened to me.

Being a millionaire before the age of 27 and losing everything before the age of 30 was my first major blow as an adult. However, there were some very valuable lessons to be learned as well. Looking internally, I really learned about my character. How did I end up in this situation? How was I treating the important people in my life before the fall and after? And, how did this happen?

How did I end up in complete financial ruin before the age of 30 after so much success? Without making excuses, I thought I was above reproach and had become arrogant. Because everything that I touched seemed to turn to gold, I thought it was all about me and that I was smarter than everyone else. In reality, I cannot blame my fall on my family, friends, associates, nor my business partners, nor even the economy. The blame falls on me.

After losing everything, I would like to tell you that I instantly learned all the lessons that I should have. However, that would be a misrepresentation of the years to follow. I went through a divorce, was better than some but worse than many at being a single father to my two daughters, and I was a poor example of being a father to my son who tragically committed suicide before I could start to build a relationship with him.

It wasn't until I understood some very simple but profound principles that I was able to put my life back together. These principles were achieved through consistent, rational thoughts and behaviors. Over the past thirty years and overcoming financial, relational, and emotional destitution, I can say that my only regrets are where I hurt people in my life.

Today, I have two daughters, three step-daughters, five son-in-laws, nine grandsons, and three granddaughters, and I cannot help but look at their lives and smile. My two daughters are married; Marci and her husband Chris have two wonderful children, Ella and Owen. And Haley is married to Jarrod with two beautiful daughters Molly and Hattie. Jennifer, my oldest step daughter is married to Dave and they have two strapping sons, Will and Sam. Elizabeth is married to Ryan (Ryan One) and they have two adoring sons Henry and Brady. And then there is Catherine that is married to Ryan (Ryan Two) and they have four incredibly different, but extremely smart sons, Andrew, Caleb, Luke and Jacob (aka Las Cuatro).

I now understand that true success is spending quality time with my children and grandchildren. During the time I am with them, everything else, including what is going on in my business or what is going on with friends or other family is out of my mind. The most important practice is not letting my thoughts be somewhere else when I am with them.

A final thought for you to think about is this. In my life, overcoming dyslexia has been easy compared to mending and repairing relationships that I took for granted and in some cases avoided entirely. I truly believe that most people who reflect on their lives would say that their biggest regrets in life would be those things that they didn't do with their family and friends instead of the things they did to them.

TWEETABLE

It's not the disorder that defines you, it's how you overcome the disorder and what you are able to accomplish to make you a better person.

Ron Jones became a real estate millionaire before age 27. After losing everything, Ron went to college for psychology and became a counselor for nine years, eventually pursuing an insurance career.

If you liked this chapter, please read Discover Your Superhero Within *which does a deep dive into understanding what it really means to be a superhero to someone, while seeing the superhero in others that you love.*

Ron is a top coach in leadership, recruiting, training, and retaining of sales teams as well as marketing and sales strategies. For a 30 minute coaching consultation, contact: rjones08@att.net / 817-734-7400.

CHAPTER 14

Victim to Victory

How I Went from Wanting to Be Dead to Loving Everything in my Head

by Contessa Akin

"Do you have a plan?" asked the lady on the other end of the phone. I was so numbed out sitting on the couch and gazing straight ahead that I didn't even realize my husband had called a suicide crisis hotline for me.

"Do you have a plan?" That one simple question turned out to be life-defining moment that changed the course of my life.

Up to that moment, I had been a victim, I experienced a wide range of adversity my entire life. At six years old, I was raped by a stranger, a rape that was facilitated by my biological mother and a rape where my half-sister guarded the door. I was betrayed by the very person who was supposed to protect me and hold me dear.

A rebel child was born that day. That abuse led to the next abuse and the abuse after that. I attached myself to guilt instead of anger, shame instead of resentment, responsibility instead of blame. The world had taught me no one could be trusted, no one could be counted on, and no one would be there for me when I needed them most.

I started acting out in big, bold ways. I hitchhiked from Texas to Los Angeles at fourteen. I did the exact opposite of anything anyone ever asked me to do. As a rebel child, the one thing I knew is that not one person or any event could ever take away my power to choose. I knew how to say "no," if not by my words then by my actions. I lived the majority of my life as a six-year-old little girl giving the proverbial middle finger to the system, my parents, and anyone who supposedly had authority over me until that life-defining moment on the couch.

That one question "Do you have a plan?" led me to more questions, which lead me to thinking differently. My thinking changed, and when my thinking changed, I found victory out of being a victim. I discovered I could be bold and strong in a different way. From that realization, I became a different sort of rebel; I rebelled with acts of self-love by changing five core beliefs. I share these five life-changing beliefs with you here.

1. Life is happening for me, not against me.

A victim mentality goes something like this:

The mentality of a victim is an acquired personality trait in which a person tends to recognize themselves as a victim of the negative actions of others and tends to behave as if this were the case even though being victimized is not a daily occurrence. In most cases, those with a victim mentality have, in fact, been the victim of wrongdoing by others, or have otherwise suffered misfortune, through no fault of their own.

Getting out of this mind trap is the first step towards victory. Being victimized does not destine you to forever being a victim. Yes, something awful happened that landed me in a terrible place. Guess what? I wouldn't change it for anything. That's right, you heard me. I wouldn't change it at all!

How many times in your life has adversity reared its ugly head and you succumbed to it? How many times did you identify with it? How many times did you hold yourself back as a result of it?

I am the woman, mother, wife, friend, and world changer I am today because of my adversities, or, shall I say, in spite of them. That's the rebel in me. I refuse to finish this life how I started it. Changing my perspective on how I engage life means I choose to honor my adversities instead of fighting them. I do not speak for every survivor, but I can say that I am grateful for my challenges. I learned how far I can be pushed and come back stronger, more resilient, and more capable than ever before.

Dare to ask yourself these questions:

What adversity have you faced? How did you (or how can you) come back stronger, more resilient, and more capable than before? Do you let those moments define you or do you define how you will use each moment?

2. The quality of my life is a direct reflection of the choices I've made so far.

If I am to be victorious, I must own my choices. The first step was for me to actively and consciously choose life, and once I did, I recognized I had the power to change. How do you choose life when life doesn't seem to want you? The answer is simple, rebel against everything that has been hurled at you! Rebel against the lies. Rebel against the pain.

Don't be defined by your real experiences.

This is the art of separating your story from the actual experience. The truth is you have faced adversities, but the lies are wrapped up in the stories you tell yourself as a result of your real experience. I learned to separate my experience into two parts: the sensational part (the visceral feelings) and the emotional part (the story associated with the experience). For example, the fact is that I was raped, and the physical pain I experienced from that rape is the sensational part. The lingering story part of that experience is me telling myself that I am not worthy of real affectionate love. I created that "I'm not worthy" story to make sense of those events.

When I kept reusing that story over and over by reframing every new event in the same old story, I was reinforcing my self-limiting beliefs. All my experiences were anchored in that false story of "I'm not good enough and the world would be a much better place without me in it."

I don't have to experience that every day. I didn't have a choice when I was victimized. I do have a choice as to whether I continue to victimize myself by re-living and re-telling myself that story.

What are the stories you tell yourself? What are the lies you are encased in?

The trouble with stories is they feel real. You find supporting evidence everywhere. Have you heard of your brain's reticular activating system and how it functions in your favor? If you decide that you have problems, then problems are all you have. If you decide you have opportunities, then opportunities are all you experience.

When you focus on something, the vacation you're going to take, the meeting you're about to walk into, the project you want to launch, that focus instantly creates ideas and thought patterns you wouldn't have had otherwise. Even your physiology responds to an image in your head as if it were a reality.

Did you catch that last line? When you have a story, your mind not only believes it, your body responds to it!

Dare to ask yourself these questions:

What is the truth in this moment? How can you choose that every day?

This is not about discounting the reality of the event, this is about not letting the story you tell yourself as a result of your experience dictate how you show up in the world.

3. Language matters.

Since I'm a life coach, a lesson I love to teach my clients is that words are just words and they have no meaning until you give it to them; words are powerful. Whenever I say that to my clients, they scratch their heads, as what I just said seems like a contradiction. Let me further explain.

When you hear something, you read something, or you overhear something, that something is just words, sounds coming out of someone else's mouth. Words have no meaning right up to the moment you give them meaning. See Webster's dictionary doesn't define what a word means to you, you do. Webster gives a definition, and when you read that definition, your life experience, your rules, and your belief systems filter that definition into something that makes sense to you. When someone else comes along and reads the same definition, they may have a different sense of what the word means to them. Words are just words.

Here is how words are also powerful and language matters. I told myself "I'm not good enough, and the world would be a much better place without me in it." I believed it. I not only believed it, remember the reticular activating system, I felt it and lived it as though it was in every fiber of my being. And to an extent, it's still there.

Did you know you will believe your own voice over all others, even if it isn't correct?

What you say to yourself has power in determining who you will be, how you will show up, how you will interpret others' words, and what you do with all that information. That is pretty powerful, isn't it? Who better than you to empower you?

I can always tell where a client is stuck just by listening to them. When they are stuck, they are insistent that I understand their version of their story. Their language reveals what they believe about themselves, what they believe about the world around them, their rules, who they think they are, how they interpret what others do and say…everything! Language matters when it comes to what you tell yourself.

Dare to ask yourself these questions:

How does the language you use affect your filters? Who are you as a result? How do you show up in the world? How can you describe the present moment without framing it in your past?

4. The opposite of courage isn't cowardice, it's conformity.

A lot of trauma has been inflicted on me by other people. How do I break the bonds of victim-abuser? How do I stand up for myself to say, "You did what you did and it no longer owns me. You don't own me!" The world can't tell me who I am to be, what I am to do, or how I am to feel. I decide who I am.

I love myself! I love my life, and no one can take that or anything from me again! By loving myself, I'm being courageous enough to be a rebel since my mind was trained to think otherwise.

Courage is more than stepping up and exerting oneself in response to extreme and immediate danger. Courage can be with us on a day-to-day basis.

Courage means taking an initiative to make a change when inactivity is the easier answer. In order to grow, we must have the courage to face truths about ourselves and have the initiative to change problems and expand our strengths.

Dare to ask yourself these questions:

Where could you use a little extra courage? What do you need? What do you stand to gain by being courageous? What do you stand to lose if you choose to crumble instead?

5. Change requires an act of rebellion.
Where is the edge of your comfort zone? Staying with what is familiar keeps us within our comfort zone. Our desire to fit in keeps us small. We adapt to the norm. We suppress our authentic selves by playing it safe.

I used to shrink and make myself feel small around others so I didn't rock the boat in order to fit in.

This conformity reinforced that crap story I shared with you earlier. I wanted to be a new type of rebel. I chose to be the kind of rebel that would make a positive difference for myself, my family, my friends, and anyone who came into my life.

I felt a prisoner to the world and to who others thought I should be. The world was trying to tell me I wasn't good enough, that I needed to shrink, that I would never amount to anything.

One day, I enlisted in the Air Force and signed up to work on airplanes. That moment felt like a little act of rebellion. I went through basic training and, boy I tell you, boot camp is no place to exercise your rebellious side, trust me. I gave it a go by asking for a quick exit. My request was denied, but somehow that moment of standing up for myself and asking for what I wanted was another little act of rebellion. Then it felt more rebellious to stay than to go since I knew my job would be something most women would not be doing.

Small, little acts of rebellion led me to work on the flight line right under our nation's most powerful air superiority aircraft, the Fighting Eagle, the mighty F-15. Every day, I felt a little more rebellious until I realized these acts of rebellion were the same as the ones before. They led me to trouble by not allowing me to realize my real self.

Fast forward all the way to the couch and that phone call and that question, "Do you have a plan?" Yes, I had a plan, I had a date, I had a time of day, and I had all the reasons why the world would be better off without me.

In that moment, I had a choice. I could listen to my language, believe what I had believed so far, and continue to conform to the past, or I could really be a rebel in a new way. I could be a rebel by saying no to my plan, no to my timeline, no to the reasons. Every single moment from that moving forward had to be rebellious moments of choosing to stand in victory.

Change requires something different from you. It will require activity. It will require you to take a flashlight and shine it in the parts of yourself that you would rather remain dark. Change will require you to rebel, to stand up, and to say "no more!"

Dare to ask yourself these questions:

Where are you playing small in your life? Who are you? What do you stand for? What do you want? What do you want to do about getting out of your comfort zone?

You wouldn't be reading this if I had stayed stuck in my story, if I had not chosen life and continued to believe the crap story. I said no to continuing to be a victim and I said yes to loving me. Are you ready to be courageous and say yes to loving you?

Dare to take the next steps from here:

1. Answer all the daring questions!

2. Be rebellious. Stay out of your comfort zone and do one thing today you've never done before!

TWEETABLE

You define how you will use adversity. Don't let adversity define you.

Contessa Akin is an intuitive life coach, world class self-love expert, firewalking instructor, and author. Due to her traumatic past, Contessa loves working with women who have experienced trauma. Her clients experience peace, scale higher heights, engage in careers of their dreams, and attract love they desire and deserve. She is wife to a Dallas Police Officer and mother of two children whom she homeschools. Find more information in Contessa's book Rebel Acts of Self-Love: How I Went from Wanting to Be Dead to Loving Everything in my Head *at www.lessonsfromadversity.com/book.*

www.lessonsfromadversity.com
Facebook: Lessons From Adversity

CHAPTER 15

Five Words that Changed My Life

by Reuben Salazar

I t was a beautiful warm sunny Southern California afternoon in August of 2008. I was sitting in my office of the aerospace welding shop that my wife and I own. My wife Anita and I were having a casual conversation as we do. We were reminiscing about how the past few years had gone.

We were grateful because we had been introduced to personal development. We attended an amazing Jim Rohn 2-Day event. Our aerospace business was on a trajectory at this point in the year to break our previous existing sales record which we hadn't come close to reaching in years. We had purchased some real estate properties as investments. Our two daughters were now married and we were starting to enjoy being "empty nesters." Our business had cash in the bank and we talked about how it was going to be great to give bonus money to our employees at the end of the year.

It seemed that we had hit our stride with everything in life. At this time, Boeing and Airbus had over 3000 planes on order each. As an aerospace supplier, this was very good news. It was a very exciting time indeed. Our employees were working six days a week to keep up with our customer's demand. However, our excitement within a month would change to disappointment, to concern, to sheer shock.

Boeing's employees went on strike in September. At first I wasn't concerned as they had done this three years prior, and the strike was resolved in a few weeks. I was sure this was going to be more of the same. Then the news came in from Wall Street; Lehman Brothers was done. Wow, this is a big institution. That turned out to be just the tip of the iceberg. More were to follow in a short time. The credit markets were frozen.

For the airline companies this meant they were not going to have the money to purchase new planes. Boeing, realizing this was happening, also had a clause with the airlines that if they had a strike that lasted more than three months, there would be no penalties for late deliveries. And the strike went on for four months. In January of 2009 the strike was over at Boeing but they were not working at the tempo they were in August of 2008.

For aerospace suppliers, many had no work. While some suppliers simply closed their doors, we were able to stay open by working three days a week until early 2009. However, the damage was done. The cash was now gone. The credit lines we had also evaporated.

Our real estate investments which we thought would be great cash flow assets for our retirement had no tenants due to the soft real estate market. No tenants meant we were paying the mortgages. The tenants never came; there were massive layoffs, and we were in the biggest recession since the Great Depression. We went through our personal money to try to keep the properties, a big mistake. By August of 2009, all of our cash reserves, business and personal, had evaporated. We could no longer pay the mortgages for our investment properties. One year later, the story had certainly changed. We were just trying to keep our house and pay the business and personal bills.

We were in danger of losing our investment properties. The banks were not willing to work out anything with investors to be able to keep investment properties, even if they were being given money to survive by the government. By August of 2010, two years after our nice, optimistic, August conversation in 2008 our investments were completely gone. The story had changed since then. Our daughters had returned home, now in the middle of divorces. We were working hard on keeping our house. We were working equally as hard to keep the business. We had also incurred debt to keep things going. Our FICO score, which was important for our ability to borrow for our aerospace welding business was trashed.

What were we going to do? At this point we had survived that hardest part. We were feeling very blessed because we knew so many that lost everything, homes, cars, and even friendships over investments deals. It was a bad time for most folks. I was so blessed to have a partner in my wife. We were able to support each other, not blaming or shaming for what happened. We understood that many of the things that had happened were completely out of our control.

By 2011 we had figured out that we were through the worse. During that year, we started to see some of the work come back. It was still slow. One of the most important things we did was surround ourselves with positive people. Our family and friends were very supportive. Some had gone through a lot worse than us.

During 2011, I attended a weeklong event put on by The Real Estate Guys™ called the Investor Summit at Sea as an event team member. This event is great because you are surrounded by positive people who are mostly entrepreneurs. While attending the event an amazing thing happened. There was an opportunity to win an hour meeting with the faculty of the event. I put a ticket in the drawing and my ticket number was called! I was shocked. What a blessing this would turn out to be. This would present an opportunity to talk to some amazing people that were playing at a high level.

I felt lost at this time in my life. I wasn't sure what direction I was going: quit the business, get a job, move to another state? (I live in California). My wife and I went into this meeting, and we had the opportunity to tell these great minds what we just had gone through. The good, the bad, and what was to me, the ugly. I was looking for a silver bullet. I was looking for magic!

All of the faculty were so supportive and empathetic. They really cared! We were touched. It was at this meeting that a gentleman by the name of Ken McElroy a Rich Dad Advisor from Robert Kiyosaki's team gave us his thoughts. He said, "Reuben, your biggest asset is your aerospace welding business. Forget any other investments for now. Focus on your business. **"Sales solves almost all problems."** Focus on increasing your sales."

Ken had given me the "silver bullet." However, at that time I did not feel like it because I wanted the pain to go away RIGHT NOW! That is not how life works. I had no idea HOW to make that happen. I was still at a loss, so I did not act on that right away. However, what he had said went into my subconscious mind and would manifest itself at the right time.

By the end of 2011 I knew I had to decide what I was going to do with the business. My heart was not completely in it. I felt pretty beat up emotionally and physically. I did blame myself for what happened. I was very disappointed with myself for what I thought were bad decisions. I had all the evidence to prove it!

By January of 2012 it was time to attend another The Real Estate Guys™ yearly event called Creating your Future™, a goal setting event, as an event team member and do my annual goal setting. It was at this event where I would make the decision as to what I was going to do business-wise: stay in business or close it.

When it came time to write business goals, something very odd happened. I closed my eyes and just let my mind wonder about the business. Then I wrote large on the piece of paper, "Work on my business, not in it." I was shocked. It was almost as if this was not written by me and I was reading what someone else wrote. (Yes, I know Michael Gerber describes this in his book *The E-myth*.) What? Where did that come from? Wow, it was clear, **"SALES SOLVES ALMOST ALL PROBLEMS."** My subconscious mind now found the opportunity and timing to help me with what Ken McElroy had advised me months ago. The HOW, suddenly came to me. I realized that "I didn't know what I didn't know." I needed to find out what I didn't know.

I wrote that I would read business books, attend business seminars, hire coaches, join masterminds with other entrepreneurs, and knew that I would have to change my mindset to one of learning, letting fears go, and trusting. I declared this to my closest confidants. I made a public declaration, which meant I would have to follow through.

I knew that this was going to cost money and time. I had plenty of time but not a lot of money. As I went out to make it happen, my wife always somehow found a way moneywise to make it happen. Within a week of making my declaration I had an email from the Brian Tracy organization that he was having a business mastery seminar in San Diego, California not far from my house, and I signed up. I knew I needed to really learn how to run a business. I had to let go of the fear of failure and fear of finding out that I wasn't doing things the best way for my business.

The seminar was great. I already had procedures for the welding side. It was clear that I would need help to get the business side working properly. I had created myself a great job. I wanted to create a business. I hired a business coach for a few months from this event and together we put together the groundwork of what I was going to do. I also knew that my mindset needed to improve. While at the Brian Tracy seminar I purchased a program that would help me with guided meditations. The gentleman that presented the keynote on mindset's name is John Assaraf. Later he would play a big part in helping me with what I didn't know. His company Neurogym helps people improve their mindset about money, business, fear, and weight loss. This program helped my mindset improve greatly.

Putting things in motion and learning and applying was starting to work. Later that year I received an email from John's company with the title: "How would you like to work on your business, not in it?" What? This is what I had written for my business goal for the year. I signed up for his program with no money to pay for it. My wife assured me that we would find it. Two weeks later I received a check from the IRS for the passive losses I had, and it covered the whole program. We were blown away. We had forgotten all about that and the money came "just in time." There is a great quote from Buckminster Fuller, "Always and just in time."

I put into action what I learned. I found out what I needed to do to create the business Ken McElroy suggested I have. It was a 3-4 year process. It was all worth it. We surpassed our best sales record within a year! We doubled our sales in just three years after hitting rock bottom. Wow, what Ken had told us, that magic moment was the catalyst to what we did. (We includes my employees; I could not have done it without their help).

It was a lot of work. Late nights, going to events, taking advice, humbling myself in the process, continually learning, and putting it into action while tweaking as necessary. Now as I write this I am waiting for my granddaughter to get home from school. I don't necessarily have to put those long hours I did when I was just trying to survive. I have been able to take time off and travel with my wife. What? Is that possible? Yes!

I want you to know, to succeed in business, or really any goal you may want to achieve, you must find out "what you don't know." Don't be afraid or too proud to find out. Find those that have already been there and can help you. You then must have the desire and the right mindset to put it into action. By putting systems and processes in place and adding strategies and tactics, I was able to gain more freedom than I ever had. I found out there were easier ways of doing things. I was stuck in what I had learned. You must continue learning, implementing, and tweaking as you go along. I did not have to do everything. You can mentor and help put a team together.

Surround yourself with positive influences and supporters. Be a supporter as well. I am privileged to be in Kyle Wilson's Inner Circle Mastermind. These amazing entrepreneurs want to help each other. They are the influencers.

I still hire coaches to help me. Most all the successful entrepreneurs continually improve themselves by surrounding themselves with the best team they can afford. I have a great team of advisors.

You never know when that magic moment will arrive, when someone may say to you something that will change your life or you read something that just clicks with you and you have that big "aha." Even when we don't realize it just happened, it happens. You just have to be open to it!

TWEETABLE

Be open to your magic moment arriving! You never know when you will find words that will click with you, giving you the aha to solve your problem.

Reuben Salazar is the President of Dan's Certified Welding Inc., a business coach, and a Certified NLP Practitioner. As a lifelong entrepreneur, Reuben has a passion to help entrepreneurs grow and achieve.

Reuben has been married to his wife Anita for over 35 years. He has 2 daughters and 3 grandchildren. Family is one of Reuben's most important values.

Reuben enjoys family life, friends, music, real estate investing, personal development and helping other entrepreneurs.

For a free 30 minute business consultation contact Reuben at thereubensalazar@gmail.com

CHAPTER 16

Persistence and Repayments

by Paul Herchman

I n 1989 at 33 years of age and early in my career I developed an idea for a company that would offer state-of-the-art medical technologies to physicians on as as needed basis allowing them to perform more advanced and minimally invasive procedures in their offices. I told a new friend, Kevin O'Brien, about it, and he wanted to join the endeavour. He quit his job, teamed up with me, and together we wrote the business plan. We needed to raise some capital. Another friend and fraternity brother from Texas Tech, Tom Montgomery, and his wife Beth, made a trip to Tulsa, Oklahoma and helped me structure Medical Alliance allowing us to raise seed capital and get started.

The company, Medical Alliance, Inc. did very well. In 1992 we were ranked the 7th fastest growing private company in Dallas. In 1994 in we were #317 in INC. 500. In 1996, at 40 years old, I led the efforts to take the company public on the NASDAQ. And in 2000 we sold to an international pharmaceutical company. It was a great success.

I was on to my next venture, and in 2003 I joined and developed a new fast-growing company called MedSurge Advances. We won some awards as a fast-growing company and created a lot of value, however it soon became apparent that I was unequally yoked with my partner. As we started becoming successful, he changed. Where once we were on the same page, I felt that his actions and philosophy related to how he wanted to run the company was not in line with my core beliefs. I was unsuccessful in completing a private equity transaction to bring in more accountability and left the company. I found myself soon entering a proxy fight and ultimately a major legal battle. I had no income and was spending big money financing legal proceedings. Then the 2008 recession hit.

I continued to try to make things happen as they always had and found, for whatever reason, I just couldn't. Up until this point in my life, if I was committed to creating a business, it just seemed to work. My businesses didn't just barely work, they worked really well. In this down phase of my life, as I kept trying to develop different startups, the failures began to add up. I was the same guy with the same work ethic, business ethics, standards, and belief in God, but for some reason now nothing was working.

My family was struggling. Thankfully we were able to sell our home in Southlake,Texas, but we lost the kids' college fund, we lost all of our savings, we lost our automobiles, and we went to live with my generous brother and sister-in-law. My wife, Donna, and I slept in my nephew's bedroom looking at his baseball trophies. My mother gave me her old car to drive and I was lucky to have it. Donna drove her mom's old car. We were barely surviving.

As the struggle continued, I had a couple of friends step up to help financially. These good friends went above and beyond the call of friendship, investing in a few of my loser start-ups and also writing us personal checks to survive. Tom Montgomery, my fraternity brother who helped me setup my first successful company, told me he was was not going to see me go into an apartment and was going to personally sign for the note on our house. He only asked that I do the best that I could do on the payments, and if I had to miss a payment, to let him know.

In 2008 I started a new company with promising medical technology imported from Belgium. I got some good friends, including Kyle Wilson, to invest, but the company was just barely making it. It was another struggle. Embarrassingly, I couldn't even pick up a meal for the family. In 2010 I bought the Christmas turkey with the little room I had left on my American Express. I had gone from very successful in business to not. At that time my wife Donna and I had been married 28 years. Donna had spent her time primarily being a devoted mom and taking great care of our kids, but suddenly our family needed any financial help she could muster. She'd been out of the workforce for 25 years. She stepped up, worked tirelessly selling men's custom clothing. On Saturdays she would go and sell bread for a company at local festivals. She said, if we could get us another $150 she would do it, and we needed it. It was hard to watch my devoted wife go out to these Saturday festivals, and my ego and confidence suffered greatly. Our new reality was shocking. Our dreams were dashed. Our mental health suffered. We even questioned our marriage and wondered if we would be better off separate. Thank God, it was a short time before we decided to lock arms and keep on going, one step at at time. I thankfully had $35 and bought Donna a ring that had inscribed in the inside band, "Faith, Hope and Love." We needed all three.

When you're down, you second guess yourself and the decisions you have made. I talked to friends and family and remember numerous people saying, "You think maybe you've already had your chance? Look where you are. You can't even support yourself or your family. You really ought to give it up: these big dreams, your entrepreneurial ideas, and just get a job. Go back into sales where you started." But I felt that God was whispering to me to have faith. He was saying, you're not finished and there is something better out there for you. Plus, I owed my friends who loaned me money and invested so much money in me. I could never pay them back if I quit now. So my search for the next opportunity continued. I was driven by fear. I had nightmares that if i wasn't successful again I would be a 75-year-old man, on the road, staying at cheap hotels trying to sell third tier medical products. That thought drove me. I was haunted by how my life had changed.

In July of 2011 Donna noticed my elbow was red and swelling. Upon her insistence, we went to the emergency room and I was diagnosed with some unknown infection. We had poor health insurance with huge deductibles and copay. I was getting sicker by the hour. Later, after I began to get better, I found out that with an infection like the one I had, you get real sick fast, hopefully get the right antibiotics, and then you get better or you die. I got better.

I was in and out of the hospital for months, and one of my daily visitors when I was in the hospital was Kevin O'Brien. We'd been competing in some form or fashion for 15 years in the same medical aesthetic marketplace since he left Medical Alliance, Inc in 1997. I quickly "re-recognized" that he's my business soulmate. We had built Medical Alliance, Inc starting in 1989, and it was our most successful company. We connected in many ways, especially on the spiritual side, and we rebooted our relationship. We were both prayerful in seeking God's direction in what we should do. I knew that I wanted to work with Kevin, but had no clear idea what we should do. At the end of 2011, Kevin came to meet with me. He said, he'd been praying and felt he was supposed to be working with me. I felt the same way.

He quit his job again and came over to work with me in a struggling healthcare venture. He told me about a new medical technology that he had discovered and that he believed could be one of the most beneficial disruptive technologies in plastic surgery. We flew to a meeting in Vancouver, performed some due diligence, and I agreed with Kevin's assessment. We felt we could develop and execute our business plan, but once again, we needed capital and we were broke. For prideful reasons I didn't want to go back to my fraternity brother, Tom Montgomery. We made efforts to raise funds, but met obstacle after obstacle. Tom was there again. When he understood that we were in danger of losing our opportunity to buy the product because we weren't getting our funding completed, he cosigned on a loan for us. Tom is one of my most successful friends, and our friendship is one example of the huge importance of keeping relationships.

By Q3 of 2012, we were up and running. We believed a device like ours which offers total control of the application of heat to human tissue would offer big benefits and disrupt other technologies in the plastic surgery industry. When you're selling products in the medical space, you can only market your product for the clearance the FDA grants. Our technology was FDA approved in the treatment of pain, using targeted heat to neutralize problem nerves in the spine. We were faced with having to work our way to market with an off-label use of this medical technology and FDA restrictions make marketing your product in that manner difficult.

Our technology was only approved for ablating nerves. We knew that we were short on funds, but deep in great relationships from our careers in the Aesthetic Medicine sector. We decided we were going to have to stay very lean in infrastructure build. We would sell product directly to physicians ourselves initially to validate the effectiveness and benefits of the technology. We would first "nail-it, then scale-it." We also recognized that in order for a technology to gain acceptance the understanding, support and influence of key opinion leader physicians was essential. We need those influencers on our side to have a chance for success.

Getting a decent valuation from financial investors for our capital raise wasn't working well, so we decided that we would only raise capital from strategic physician investors who understood the benefits of our technology. We felt that physicians who saw what this technology could do would also understand the valuation of our company. We began to sell them the product at a discount. We were raising money from physicians who believed in us and our vision. In Q3 and Q4 of 2012, our first year, we recorded about a million dollars in revenue and actually had a small profit.

At trade shows we didn't have the best FDA clearance to market the product clearly. We had a small booth and promoted that we were organizing doctors who wanted to play a part in developing this new disruptive technology by joining our clinical advisory council. We also would award physicians stock options in exchange for clinical work. To our benefit, since we were raising capital, we needed to disclose all the relevant information about the company, including our clinical development strategy to potential investors. At trade shows we didn't prominently display that we were selling technology; we promoted that we were raising capital. We had physicians with express interest in investing sign non-disclosure agreements, and we were able to fully share with them the details regarding what we believed the technology would do, how it could do it, and where we thought the company was going. All potential investors need full disclosure to make an educated decision about investing.

In 2013 we added another key executive named Mike McDonald. Mike joined us as our CFO to insure proper financial reporting, analysis and projections, and documentation operations as well as work with us in the capitalization of the company. We were growing and ended up recording about five million dollars in revenue in 2013. That's five times 2012 revenues. In 2014 we booked approximately 11 million dollars in revenue. We were recognized in the Dallas 100 as the seventh fastest growing private company in Dallas, the same award Kevin and I had won in 1992. It was surreal to be back at the podium together 14 years later accepting the same award.

We also strongly felt that you should compensate people for the contributions they make to your company. If you have cash you can pay them, or if you don't you can use options as compensation. These option holders worked hard for our company.

Kevin and I knew we couldn't afford to blow this opportunity. When I was younger I was more aggressive and I didn't execute exit opportunities when I should have. I learned that when things are going well, your investors and shareholders typically want more. The more valuable the company becomes, the more you want, and soon full fledged "gold fever" infects the team. You hold out for more and more and miss the timing. It was very important that when Kevin and I started the company, we agreed on what a financial win would look like. We shook hands with the understanding that the minute we can sell the company and clear five million each to hit our goal, we sell.

When we got to a $24 million valuation, Kevin and I had met our initial financial goal of clearing $5 million each. We felt even better about the ongoing practice of awarding options to create more value. The cherry on top was in February of 2016 when we sold our company for an enterprise value of $83 million.

We needed lots of people to help us, to work with us, to even have chance to build a successful company. We didn't have the cash to pay them. We used our options as our currency. We got some of the best talent in all aspects of the company and began building a dedicated and strong sales team. Everyone across the company didn't make much cash compensation at first, but our sales team began to make some really good commissions and we began to share the wealth. When we sold the company we had over 50 physician investors and 200 option holders to whom we happily distributed the money.

I saw that, at some point soon, I was about to be in the position to repay those who lent money to me to help us survive and I could repay them using shares of my personal stock. They ended up getting three to four times their money. The cool thing is that through all of this, none of these men ever made me feel overburdened or under pressure. That says something about them. I worked to stay in touch and keep them informed, and then this amazing success occured. Selling the company and returning their money multiplied was a great joy. I felt great taking care of them as they had me. Now my family is taken care of for generations and our first investors made up to eight times their money. The last round investors made about a two times return in a short period of time.

As we were building the company we became very aware of God's hand on our business. Good things simply happened to us that were beyond our control. For the last 10 years it seemed that when the storms would hit, I was thrown into the rocks and whatever little boat I was building was crushed by the rocks. But not this time. When the storms hit and the winds would blow, they blew in a new direction. That new direction was always better.

We learned to be so faithful seeing that the things we needed were coming to us just in time. Not typically early, but just in time. Over all these years, it was an amazing journey of faith. I've kept this Bible verse in my wallet since mid 2013.

> Ecclesiastes 9:11
>
> *I returned and saw that under the sun, that the race is not to the swift, nor the battle to the strong, neither yet bread to the wise, nor yet riches to men of understanding, nor favor to men of skill, but time and chance happeneth to them all.*

Through my failures I learned a lot. There are countless things that could have happened that could have destroyed our company. For some reason, none of it happened to us. I don't know why we were blessed in this way, but we were. For generations my family is going to be in good shape financially. To go through the really bad times I found that we all emerged with a different perspective and have more understanding and compassion. I can better understand how a few bad things in a row can change one's course in life. Thank God I had family and friends to help me stop the fall.

I could have just gone back into sales somewhere to earn a nice living, but I didn't feel like I could do that because I owed too much money to people I cared for. I had an obligation to pay it back. If you stay in the game, you have a chance. Keep trying.

One of my biggest lessons is don't quit. Adapt, but don't quit. If you're not in the game, on the field, you have no chance of scoring.

TWEETABLE
If you're not in the game, on the field, you're not going to score.

Paul R. Herchman, Jr is a proven growth-oriented entrepreneurial executive offering years of experience in the conception, development and implementation of medical/aesthetic services and devices. He has lead several well known and successful start-up companies from start-up to shareholder exit. With solid business insights with the ability to raise capital, analyze market needs, envision new program concepts, and strategize, Paul excels in devising non-traditional solutions that exploit emerging technologies or trends.

pherchmane911@gmail.com

LinkedIn: Paul Herchman

CHAPTER 17

Starting Over On My Own Stage

by April Krahl

I had to do something I swore I would never do in my life. Divorce. What an ugly, terrible thing. I'd never wish this upon anyone. I went into this marriage never wanting it to end, but towards the split, it was all that I could do to move on with my life. I had invested so many years with this person and now had a child in the midst of it all.

I truly wanted it to work, but there just was no communication. Even after the first few years, I could not fathom it ever ending. Friends thought we had the perfect marriage and strived to be like us. A very good friend who knew us both very well told me that if our marriage ended, then there was no hope for marriage itself. The person that I had married and loved for so many years had changed, and I did not know him anymore. He often heard me saying, "I don't know who you are, but I want my husband back." I knew that in my heart I could not spend any more time waiting for change.

Making this decision was one life-defining moment. It came with many unknowns of my future. Knowing that I had to make this decision impacted my child, impacted my life, and impacted the business I spent years growing. This was my life and all that I knew.

We had built a business together, and I was the majority owner. It had grown into a large seminar company with corporate sponsors and a trade show. I'd hire keynote speakers such as Daymond John and Brian Tracy to open up certain events. Attendees flew in from all over the US to be there. I was concerned that this was in jeopardy.

The last couple of year's felt impossible. I was working all the time running the business and was solely taking care of our toddler son. I hardly saw my friends because I worked so much, and by the time I had any down time I just wanted to relax. Everyday seemed like a battle, and I felt like I was walking on eggshells in my own home that last year. Nothing I ever did was appreciated or good enough. I'd work and bring in all our money for it to be spent, and then have to do it all over again. I felt like a hamster on a wheel with no end in sight.

After many attempts at counseling there was still no communication or solution. All the times I tried to talk, I felt like I was speaking to a wall. I had to do something I never wanted to do. I filed for divorce. I did this to protect myself but to also get his attention that we had a problem. I thought it would be a wakeup call to start communicating with me. It was not. As soon as I filed, it became a game of war. It was a nightmare for me. Business accounts were changed, funds were flying out of accounts against standing orders, and I was getting nowhere in court even after paying thousands of dollars in attorney fees. I never expected it to be like this. I figured we could be civil and have some resolve. I thought that after so many years together he would want the best for my son, me, ultimately, us. I was wrong and stood alone. All I wanted was to be happy. I felt like I was screaming and no one could hear me. My goal for my immediate future was peace and happiness. At the time it was nowhere in sight but it was something I strived to attain.

After filing, I was left with no earning potential. I was the majority owner, but the accounts had been taken over and passwords were changed. I had to solely support my son and keep a roof over our heads. Funds were running short with all the attorney fees, plus the business and personal expenses I was paying; I had to do something and do it quick. When the accounts were unlawfully taken over and nothing was done with them, I knew I had to do something.

So I opened up my own company and completely started over with a brand new name.

I was very nervous starting a new business name in this male-dominated industry. Potential customers had always tested my knowledge before, and I had to gain their trust in order for them to buy from me in the past. I succeeded and felt confident under my other brands, but this was a new endeavor. Since our company started by changing the industry with specialized sales training, we had a lot of copycats. Some had been to our events and tried to "re-teach" what they learned at ours. Others, completely copied our model which took trial and error and years to perfect. I had taken a big risk with an endeavor I created, the IRC Summit, which was a major success. Now, I was starting over.

I was concerned because I knew so many of my potential clients looked at new training companies in this industry with a slanted eye, as most failed or offered something they could not actually deliver. I didn't want to start over again in an industry where my company had been a staple, where I had grown and done so well. I helped pave the way for these copycats that used my ideas to benefit themselves and took credit for them. This was a huge concern for me.

I had lot of customers and corporate sponsors from the other brands I created in the past, but I was concerned no one would recognize my new name and look with a slanted eye at a new company. I had remained very quiet about the separation out of mutual respect. Then I started receiving calls from business associates checking on me to make sure I was alright and wanted to know what I was going to do with the business moving forward. They were concerned as much as I was. I appreciated their support and the courage they gave me to keep on doing what they believed I was great at doing.

I went to work out of necessity. It was sink or swim, and I was the only one who was going to take care of my son and myself. I had started a few businesses in the past, so the setup was easy, but making myself mentally strong was difficult.

My life had just done a 180. I was starting over, living by myself with just my son. I had friends but zero family in the same state. Many thought that I may move to be by my family. That was never my plan and not having my family here was very difficult for me. My son had to look up to me, so I did my best to remain strong and make sure that his life did not change. On another spectrum, I had to start a new business and make it work so that we could keep a roof over our heads.

To make myself mentally strong, I prayed a lot. There were so many days that I did not want to get out of bed. I knew myself and knew that if I let myself slip just one day that I could easily slip into depression. I was already down and mentally beat up. I didn't want that extra slump, so no matter how I felt, I never slept in—not even one day. There were so many days that I almost talked myself into not moving. Laying in bed felt so great. I was tired, beat down, and needed rest, but I knew I had to get up. I had a son. I had a future, and I had done it in the past, and I could do it again. I had to tell myself to mentally trick myself into knowing that I could do it again. I had previously heard Tony Robbins say that motion creates emotion. So each day no matter how I felt, I got up. I went to my office and forced myself to create this new company. It was a constant battle of the mind.

Setting up my new endeavor was easy, getting it launched with a new site and people I had been working with for years was easy. This time though, I reached out to new speakers who I had never worked with before. They told me they were honored to speak at my event, and I was relieved and grateful. Getting paid was another story. I had previously had unlimited credit with merchant accounts. I applied for new accounts and asked them to see my past accounts, letting them know it was still me but a new brand. That didn't matter. I felt like a 18-year-old high school student applying for a credit card for the first time. My past merchant accounts were corporatized. They saw my past activity, it was unlimited, but as a new entity I was treated as a nobody. I had started my new company, but I was being held back as to how I could actually receive funds.

I launched my first seminar under my new brand. I was very nervous. My funds had been exhausted on attorneys. I had spent years building up a savings, and poof! It was gone. I was starting over from scratch, and it felt awful.

After it was launched it was like nothing changed. My customers never asked about the new name and non-customers who ended up purchasing never questioned the new brand either. They had been receiving marketing and checking out what had been happening before.

I was selling, but my merchant accounts flagged me for bringing in funds too quick with a new account. They held 75% of my funds until my seminar was over! This caused a lot of stress and problems, because I needed the funds that were already paid to me in order to make the seminar happen. I pushed on and got through it, but it seemed like as soon as I got over one hurdle another one popped up. I finally was getting funds I needed to live on and to operate a business. Where was my break? Other risks could have easily popped up too, in hindsight, but luckily, early on I became great at negotiating with hotels and was able to mitigate any of those potential risks. The merchant accounts blindsided me though. At the time each hurdle was devastating, but I knew if I had gotten this far then I could get to the next level.

I sold my first event out by myself under a new brand, in a new venue, and had to close registration. That was a turning point for me. I had been doing it on my own the entire time, but hadn't realized my potential when I was working with my husband. I had put myself in the background. I now had to get on stage and speak too. I had always wanted to speak but was so busy running the business, doing the marketing, and selling out the events that I only got up on stage in spurts. Now I not only had to set it up but I had to speak as well. It scared the hell out of me at first. I once read that most people would rather die than get up on stage and speak in front of an audience. I thought that was very intimidating. As a woman, I am judged from the beginning in a male-dominated industry. No pressure, right? Attendees have continued to come back and have recommended my company, so I must be doing something right. I do, however, continue to work on my speaking and making events better each time.

I went on to do other events with many five-star Facebook reviews and happy attendees who gained knowledge to better their businesses and themselves. No one ever sees the process, the risk, the sleepless nights, the sweat, the tears, the hurdles behind creating something of value that truly is aiming to help others succeed. They only see the event and experience the event. My goal is to make that event a life changing moment for them. To show them others have done it, there's a plan, and they can achieve it too.

Time is a four letter word. It can be for or against you. Use it wisely. If you're in a bad relationship, whether it be marriage or business, use some of your time to make it right. If you're spending too much time trying to make it work, then move on. I've learned it's easier to start over than to hold on to the things of the past that only weigh you down. When the door closes, don't try to force it open. Focus on the right door opening.

Once I tasted respect, I never wanted to go back. Happiness and peace have been my goals. I enjoy helping others succeed. Money comes and goes. Time is inevitable. You can always make more money, but you can't buy time. Live life to its fullest and find out what gives you peace and happiness. In business, do what you are good at and work hard at it. You reap what you sow. If you want to be successful in a certain business or career, put your hand to the plow and never look back. You have to put in the work. It takes time, patience, dedication, and faith, but if you do it right, time is on your side. Above all, never give up. Spend your time wisely and invest in what makes you happy.

If you're in a marriage that is heading south, do what you can to go back to why you got married in the first place. Communication and respect is key. Do whatever you can to save it. Go to counseling. If it does not work, then do your best to be civil and move on. Still treat the other person how you would want to be treated. If children are involved, love them and make them know that they are loved. Keep their life the way they are used to living it. Be positive and respect the mother or father in front of the children. Build your children up and let them know that they can do anything they set their mind to. Put God first and all things will fall into place.

TWEETABLE

It's easier to start over than to hold onto the past that weighs you down. Failure really is the opportunity to start over, only this time greater.

April Krahl is a visionary, creator, trailblazer, and the founder of Storm Consultants, LLC & the IRC Summit. She has been helping storm restoration contractors succeed through live training and educational events since 2011. April is a certified Brian Tracy Sales Trainer and a self-motivated professional in business consulting, market strategy, advertising, promotion, pricing, and sales and an expert in new marketing concepts, launching new products, and executing events with precision.

Aprilkrahl@gmail.com
www.linkedin.com/in/aprilkrahl

CHAPTER 18

Life, Love, Death, and Decisions in the Balance

by Michael Brownell

My initial response was to smirk and chuckle, but as we maintained eye contact, I could sense there were more layers. Still, it was pretty funny, and I knew that was part of the message. First, find the joy.

Then, understand that big decisions and poignant moments are a fundamental part of life, so it's better to face them with a positive, balanced perspective rather than fear. Try to view events and issues as authentically and constructively as possible. Those weren't the words he said, but that's how I came to understand their meaning over time. Wisdom takes time to seep in, and facing the bigness of life requires clarity. This was me realizing a new level of adulthood. A defining moment.

Going outside for some fresh air and a break from the sterile cool of the hospital room, I pondered this most recent father-son discussion. Like many of our one on one talks, it didn't set out to be proverbial but somehow found its way there through the path of wit and circumstance. I was so grateful for our history and that we had been able to bridge from the father-son relationship of my youth to one between men. And I was sad that these talks would likely soon end, which added to the impact of his words.

There were several reasons for this visit to see Dad. One was based on life and death, as he was in serious condition. Another was based on love, as I was planning to propose marriage and wanted his counsel. And we always ended up talking about our careers, which I really looked forward to since I was still relatively early in mine. All together it was a lot to process and I was struggling, searching for how to think about the big decisions and moments in life.

When presented with my desire to ask Nancy to marry me and a request for his advice, Dad looked at me for a long moment.

"I've been married three times so I'm not sure you want my advice..." he said with a twinkle in his eye.

"Well, you must have learned something." I replied, egging him on a bit.

That hung in the air for a time and then he said, "Son, you have a basic choice to make in marriage and in life, you can be right or you can be happy. Choose wisely"

> *The right word spoken at the right time is as beautiful as gold apples in a silver bowl.*
> (Proverbs 25:11)

That was the first time I'd ever heard that bit of wisdom. Now you can find quotes and commentary almost too easily on the web, but this was 1993, and the Google search engine wasn't invented yet. Perhaps this was first uttered around a campfire in ancient times by our ancestors. Doesn't matter. What was so impactful to me was how and when I heard the concept, and that I was open and ready to understand it and learn.

It's a clever and interesting way to think about making life choices. A thoughtful approach to balancing challenging decisions between two positives: being right and being happy. It was comical and true with respect to the "happy wife, happy life" meme, but also very insightful with regard to choices, relationships, and life. It wasn't so much an either/or option but a perspective on balanced decision making. The key, it seems, is in the balance.

This principle applied very early in my engagement to Nancy. We lived in different cities and both had professional careers, so we had to decide who would move and change jobs when we married. My analytical mind began producing lists of pros and cons and looking for the right answer. This caused some conflict as we both had ideas for what was right, and I was pretty career driven.

When I realized that us being happy with how and where we initially planted our family was far more important than me trying to be right, the decision became clear. I relocated. It just made the most sense in the big picture even if it wasn't clear what my next career move would be.

Happy doesn't always mean smiley and jolly. It can mean harmony and peace and agreement. Looking at hard decisions as an opportunity is healthy.

Over time a trend has developed where we use this principle to put family first and find creative and effective ways to adapt our professional lives. We both make changes. This works for us, and the principle provides a flexible decision making tool. This advice has helped us have 23 years of happy marriage and a loving family, while also having a significant impact on our professional lives.

As a young executive and entrepreneur I also found this balanced approach to decision making highly valuable. Laser vision correction via the Lasik procedure was really taking off in the mid-2000s and Intralase Corp. was experiencing tremendous growth. We had developed an innovative femtosecond laser that made precise and safe incisions in the eye and had become a new standard in Lasik and corneal eye surgery. I was Vice President of Product Development, ran the R&D group, and collaborated with a wide range of people, companies, and customers.

We were way out in front in the market, our product offering and pipeline were robust, and we were crushing it. We were doing the right things right, and in fact that was a corporate core value and a process we had integrated into how we operated. As a company we were striving for and finding that balance in our decision making. Ultimately this lead to us being acquired for $800 million dollars, demonstrating that doing the right things right can in fact make all parties happy.

Some years later I was in an executive role at an early phase technology company, with broad technical and leadership responsibilities. We were raising funds, developing new products, and growing our business. A situation arose where I had to look deeply at my values and principles, and I faced some very difficult decisions about what to do. In this case, the focus had to be on what I felt was right, which would cause significant impact to the happy factor. But because of this right vs happy concept, I was able to see clearly that doing the right thing based on my values and principles compensated the struggle my family and I would face with the resulting stress and changes.

I was able to avoid a lot of internal negativity and stress with this insight. Many different types of bad things happen in life. Realizing that I needed to be clear on where my boundaries were and behave accordingly was powerful. Soon after, I left the company and that lead to great new opportunities, for all the right reasons. And we ended up happy once again.

Over time I became an active investor in areas like cash flowing real estate and private equity deals. These investments inevitably contain difficult situations and decisions. We can all be confrontational and competitive when the stakes are high. Our egos can demand us to be "right" even when this negatively impacts a given situation. The right decision does not automatically equate to someone being right. Finding the balance in each situation is essential.

That was one of my last deep and real moments with my dad, but it produced a lifetime of insight in my relationships, my family, and my career. It's all about balanced decision making and authentically looking at what is "right" and the conditions for being "happy." Even in the defining moment of my father's death I was able to see that our relationship was right and we were happy, through that one simple phrase. My hope is that you will find that balance as well in the big moments in your life.

TWEETABLE
In life you have a basic choice, to be right or to be happy. Choose wisely.

Michael and Nancy Brownell continue consulting in their professional fields as well as making lifestyle investments and sponsoring syndications in income producing real estate. These investments now include vacation property, coffee farms, apartments, and senior housing. They welcome opportunities to connect with like-minded people who are interested in investing alongside them for passive cash flow and lifestyle freedom. Reach Michael at michael1brownell@gmail.com, on Facebook, or LinkedIn.

CHAPTER 19

A Moment at Mayo

by Louis B. Cady, M.D.

"**Y**R U Sick?**"** is the customized license plate that the provocative Cady Wellness Institute naturopath, Dr. Whitney Gabhart, ND, has threatened to place on her car. It's also a really good question. An even broader question is "Why are you not feeling well?" or "What's got you feeling down?" or the request "Tell me more about your problems with concentration (or fatigue)."

From a human-interest point of view, and as an expert in the integration of mind and body for peak performance, I have found it absolutely fascinating to listen to the narratives that our patients tell us when they arrive at Cady Wellness Institute. Here are a few of my favorites:

- "I've been to lots of doctors and they all tell me that my labs are fine."

- "My son went to the doctor for his ADHD and (take your choice)

  - totally lost his appetite where he lost 5 lbs in a week;

  - he looked like a drugged zombie;

  - he was acting like a crazy man when his medication wore off;

  - he became mean, spiteful, and angry—like a demon child;

  - he was tic'ing like crazy."

- "Doctor, I don't know what's wrong. All my doctors say that I'm depressed, but no antidepressant is working for me."

- "Doc, I feel like since my late 40s my mojo is gone. I just can't get moving or excited about anything."

- "There's just something wrong with my brain. Something's different. My doctor says I'm depressed. But none of the drugs are working."

- "Doctor, one day in my 40s I realized that I was fading. And then, in a few years, I got tired, depressed, couldn't lose weight, felt like a slug, couldn't sleep, and had no sex drive. My husband is complaining. I'm starting to have hot flashes. But I've been to the doctor and she says all my labs are fine, I'm not menopausal, and it's just middle age."

All of these patients—with all of these miseries—have been looking for an identification of a problem as well as a solution. They are not getting it with medical care as it is currently being practiced in this country. From doctor to doctor, these suffering men and women are told: "There's nothing wrong with you," or "You just must have a touch of depression," or "Welcome to middle age. This is the way you're supposed to feel." Sometimes women patients are told, "You just need to lose some weight. Go diet and exercise." or, more therapeutically, but not at all more guaranteed to work, "Here, just take this antidepressant."

The tragedy is that all of these case histories have, at root cause, a *biological* problem in the patient's physiological system that is destabilizing him or her. Conventional Western medicine is not casting a diagnostic net wide enough to pick up subtle inadequacies in lab values. And rarely is functional medicine testing done. People are suffering as a result.

Once Upon a Time in America, or Actually...TEXAS

I grew into maturity in northeast Texas with a local population that could best be described as "the good ol' boys." In a community where football was the sport the cool kids played and my friends idolized the best players, I was labeled as the "nerd boy that played piano." But I loved my piano. And I loved my music. So I happily played it while thinking about a potential career in medicine. Unfortunately for me, in high school I did not do well in math (or chemistry) and, despite an interest in becoming a physician, I decided that I was not cut out for it and my career path diverted into six years of musical study with undergraduate and graduate degrees in performance from the Conservatory of Music at the University of Missouri, Kansas City. Then, on the other end of six years of college work, there were absolutely no job prospects available.

Through a chain of remarkable circumstances, I found myself competent in science and math, then in medical school, and then in residency in psychiatry at the Mayo Clinic in Rochester, MN.

While at Mayo, one of my life-defining moments occurred. One of my consultants at Mayo, Dr. John A. Graf, MD, and I were talking about some fine point of psychopharmacology pertaining to one of our patients. Dr. Graf was considered one of the most brilliant consultants in the department of psychiatry at Mayo.

That memorable morning in 1992 or 1993, I asked Dr. Graf that medication question. He paused and looked up at me. Then, in that basso profundo voice I will never forget, and with the famous twinkle in his eye, he slowly and ponderously intoned (as was his style), "Well, I don't know Dr. Cady. We should go check the literature." And we did: on a computer with dial-up, pre-Windows, pre-Mac, pre-Apple, pre-WYSIWYG technology.

This idea struck me as remarkably different. Up until that time, my entire world had revolved around the framework that if you didn't know the answer to the question for your homework, you looked it up in your textbook(s). Nowhere else. You didn't need to.

Dr. Graf's perspective was different. This wasn't looking in a textbook. It was casting your net of intellectual inquiry out across the entire world and to every piece of medical research that had been published and catalogued up until that time. For me, this was an *immediate* paradigm shift. Indeed, in my experience at Mayo up until that time, this was the first I had ever heard a consultant actually admit that he or she didn't know everything and that a final authority beyond him or her should be consulted.

Secondly, this drove home to me that even if you were at the top of your game and on staff at one of the most prestigious medical institutions in the country, you still couldn't possibly be expected to know it all. This was enormously freeing to me. I would no longer have to expect myself to walk around with every possible fact and statistic crammed into my brain like I had been doing to prepare for all those tests in medical school.

The third, and the most impactful, point of learning was that of Dr. John Graf's intellectual humility. If he didn't know the answer, he would admit it. After he admitted his ignorance, he would remedy it. And then, most profoundly and most importantly, he would submit his opinions and conjectures to the overwhelming evidence of the body of the entire world's peer-reviewed literature.

THEN versus NOW

Once upon a time in this country, you had a family physician. This was someone you knew well, and who knew you, your family, and your circumstances. He or she could refer you to a specialist if needed.

As opposed to Mayo Clinic in its golden age, however, the practice of primary care medicine in this country at present is based neither on the strength of the world's peer-reviewed medical literature nor the core Mayo concept that "the needs of the patient come first." Current medical practice is, in fact, now based on the following inescapable realities:

- The length of time allowed for a patient-physician encounter is shrinking. 15 minute "new patient appointments" are getting cut to 7 minutes. Or 7½ minutes if you're lucky.

- Your body is getting farmed out to the specialists. Nobody knows everything about you any more.

- If you have to go to the hospital, your primary care is temporarily and immediately severed with your family doctor or primary health care provider and taken up by "the hospitalist," who is someone who doesn't know you, your history, your background, or what makes you tick as a person.

- School physicals are now done at Wal-Mart "Quick Clinics" instead of at a family physician.

- The dreaded "EMR" (electronic medical record) has arrived on the scene. These programs are designed to reflexively demand "practice guidelines" recommendations be implemented rather than thoughtful, common sense medical practice or doing what the peer-reviewed medical literature demands.

But even this is not the darkest and most devastating factor in the destruction of medical care.

The Fourth Great Crossover
Dan Sullivan, the right brained, genius entrepreneur and business coach who founded the organization The Strategic Coach, has been talking about the four great crossovers in human history for at least two decades. His book, The Great Crossover, was published in 1997.

According to Dan, the first great crossover in human history was the development of language. The second crossover was writing, the third was the printing press, and the fourth great crossover is now upon us, "The Age of the Microchip."

The resultant changes in medical practice have been insidious. Most people know that computers are used in almost all offices these days for calendaring and scheduling. EMRs are no surprise as you watch your health care provider's eyes glaring at their screens. What is not known to you is what is getting served up to the "provider" on those screens.

Previously, doctors and clinicians were given the "normal ranges" on blood work reports for *all the age ranges* of a man or woman. If one looked carefully, and thought about it for a second, one could see that the "normal" hormone ranges went *down* with age.

128

Now, however, thanks to the wonders of the microchip and its almost unlimited processing power, the hospital or lab computers, which are in charge of printing out lab values, can decide what the clinician will be shown. No longer does (s)he get all the normal ranges. What is printed out is only the so-called "normal" range of hormone levels for the patient's age. And the computer knows how old you are because it's got your birthdate. And the "normal ranges" are decided, pretty much, "by committee." In other words, if you are older, you don't *deserve* to have hormone and other lab values consistent with optimal health at a younger age.

And then there's the matter of how the "normal ranges" are calculated for any age group. Essentially, if you are within 2.5% to 97.5% of the population's values *for your age* you are considered "normal." In point of fact, your lab values could be at the third percentile level, and you would still be considered "normal."

The question is, do you want your labs to be "normal" (within the reference range) or "optimal?" If you are a fatigued, obese, depressed, brain-fogged man or woman staggering into your appointment with your doctor, are you really going to be comforted with the reassurance that "Good news, your thyroid labs are all within the normal range?" Or, what if you are an andropausal, fatigued, middle-aged guy who has lost your mojo—as well as your erectile capabilities—and have been told, "Good news, your testosterone is normal."

Guess who (or what) prints out those "normal" labs. Yep, the computer. And these labs are adjusted for your "age group." Without thinking.

Interestingly, the peer-reviewed literature for medicine pretty much speaks with one voice when you start digging into each hormone and where optimum levels would be. Typically, the higher (within reason) your values are, the better, even if this puts them in a range that "should be" for a younger person—perish the thought. Study after study after study has been done showing the benefits of higher levels of testosterone, estradiol, progesterone, DHEA, and even growth hormone (although this last one is controversial).

I Lived It, I Learned It, You Got It

I have given you the intellectual and statistical background for some of the concepts already advanced. But what changed a conventionally trained, conventionally practicing, totally allopathic psychiatrist into this veritable zealot for functional medicine and "optimization of the biological platform?"

The first point of inflection was that momentous comment casually dropped by Dr. Graf.

Then, from 1993 to 2002, I practiced medicine by essentially "picking the low hanging fruit." The cases that came to me from other doctors or from self-referral were pretty easy. In the early 2000s, however, I began realizing that I couldn't get all of my patients well. (And we had begun attracting "end of the line" cases by that time.) The medications, even if they were supposed to be working, simply weren't. It was like there was "something else" wrong with the patients. I just didn't know what it was.

From 2002 up to the present, I have been fascinated with the application of new concepts of age management medicine and hormonal optimization and have avidly pursued education in it. Those new concepts come back to our practice at Cady Wellness Institute for the betterment of our patients' lives. I've learned it, and I have been teaching it nationally and internationally.

In 2005, I was also introduced to a remarkable piece of technology: a laser driven Raman spectrophotometer that could read out a person's antioxidant levels in two minutes, painlessly, through something called the Raman shift. I had to have it. And I did. The impact of this device on my patients' health has been profound. The immediate determination of antioxidant level gives me an instant "read" of the patient's nutritional status, and we can then set about rebuilding the patient by addressing his or her nutrient deficiencies, as well as all other deficiencies we find on conventional lab testing.

The NeuroVitality® Breakthrough

Some years ago, I set down the step-by-step procedures used at Cady Wellness Institute to get people well, and not just "better." It is our registered NeuroVitality® trademarked process.

The first part is a massive data gathering operation where the patient fills out extensive background information. Secondly, the two hour NeuroVitality® Interview elicits all the relevant details of a patient's history. The third component is what we call Body Systems Diagnostics™, which is an exhaustive laboratory evaluation of a patient's physiology using conventional labs, functional labs, and nutritional testing. On average, our lab workup is 3-5 times more comprehensive than what our patients have experienced from their other physicians.

We integrate established concepts from the peer-reviewed medical literature—exactly as I learned from Dr. Graf—and then loop back around and start rebuilding the patient from the ground up. Let me leave you with these concepts.

- There are a number of physical issues that can make you appear that you have mental issues. These include hypothyroidism, hypoadrenia ("adrenal fatigue"), sex hormones that are not optimal, nutrient deficiencies, and undiagnosed sleep disorder problems.

- The solution is not an antidepressant for your "depression." The solution is, rather, to fix the underlying medical issues.

Moments that Can Define Your Life

As I think back across my career—the hundreds of lectures I've heard, the training I've had, and the peers and mentors I have known—Dr. Graf's intellectually humble and casual comment has had the most significant impact on my life, our practice at CWI, and the lives of the thousands of patients we have treated.

Dr. Graf's touchstones of humility are relevant across all fields of human endeavor: you can't be expected to know it all. You must seek out wise counsel and relevant sources. You must be humble. And you must be diligent.

TWEETABLE

You can't be expected to know it all. You must seek out wise counsel and relevant sources. You must be humble. And you must be diligent.

Dr. Louis Cady is the founder and CEO of Cady Wellness Institute in Newburgh, IN, focused on integrating mind and body for peak performance. Dr. Cady not only treats the sick back to health, but also focuses on helping children and adults achieve total wellness and optimum levels of performance. He specializes in difficult or seemingly hopeless to treat cases of mental health and flagging levels of energy.

He is a Diplomate of the American Board of Psychiatry & Neurology and a Fellow of the American Psychiatric Association.

www.cadywellness.com
@LouisCadyMD
(office) 1-812-429-0772

CHAPTER 20

On Not Being Enough

by Takara Sights

With last call behind us, we loitered on the orange-lit curb outside a bar in downtown Los Angeles. A bearded, blue-eyed man with a sheepish smile introduced himself. He was from Canada. "I'm Canadian!" I delivered with an enthusiastic high-five. A few minutes of conversation later, our Uber arrived.

In the car, "Ima need you to stop," said my friend from the front seat. "Why are you always so excited about telling people you're Canadian but not about the fact that you're Black?"

For once in my life, I was prepared with a quick comeback in spite of, or perhaps enabled by, the buzzing of my head. I said, "If I just found out I was Black, I would be telling people about that too." She returned to conversation with her coworkers beside me and let it rest.

Despite all appearances, this moment was not something I brushed off. It burrowed into my chest and roused other insecurities I had tucked in there. I thought about it a lot over the next few days.

I was born biracial. My dad is a white Canadian American. My mom is an African American. As a person who has roots in two worlds, more often than not I feel like I don't belong in either.

Per the one drop rule, I can never be White. Among other things, my giant, richly curly hair, big butt, thick thighs, and tan skin make it obvious.

At the same time, in Black communities, I am definitely light-skinned. I grew up in a house that spoke and I now speak in a "standard American accent." I don't know the names of most hip hop artists or rappers. I don't like sports. I don't always know the newest dance moves. I've never lived in a predominantly Black neighborhood until now. I eat salad regularly, ride my bike with my dog, and wear ugly, dirty, worn-out sneakers. As I understand, that's some pretty White shit to do. So, Black people (sometimes other people too, but mostly Black people in my experience) say I'm White on the inside. This has been pointed out to me my whole life.

People have societal expectations around what it means to be Black. If you don't act the "right" way or know the "right" things, you don't fit in. And we all want to fit in somewhere. We all want to belong.

When this "not Black enough" insecurity surfaced in me, I was very concerned. I want to be Black enough. Being Black is part of me. My family is Black, my hair is Black, my experiences are Black, I am Black. But, if other people can't tell, maybe I'm not doing it right.

I thought maybe I should go back to spending intentional time studying music videos and making sure I read historically significant Black books. I have gone through fervent bouts of making sure I know about my culture. I truly think it is important to learn about, appreciate, and understand the people you come from. Ignorance is not to be forgiven. We all must participate in our communities because together we are strong. Please understand, I am not excusing dismissal of identity. I never meant to put my studying, my intentional integration into Black culture, aside, but we can only have one priority.

With these thoughts heavy on my mind, I emailed my mom. First, I wrote a long one. It was one o'clock in the morning and I ended up with over two pages. *Should I try harder to be Blacker? Do I not have enough pride in my identity as a Black woman? Have I been too busy putting being queer, being Canadian, being American, being in my twenties, being a gentrifier, being an author, first?*

It all felt too dramatic to send to Mom, so I distilled it down...into one question. *Mom, has anyone ever told you you're not Black enough?*

Her response was perfect. Did I ever tell you about the kids who wouldn't be friends with me and my sisters because we lived in a white neighborhood? I, and your aunts, have all felt the same way. Be who you are. That's all anyone who loves and cares about you can ask. Imperfection is a gift. I love you.

Waking up to this message, I was in tears. The truth is, we don't choose to put any identity over another, we are all of our identities at once. I am as Black as I am. And that is enough.

I wholeheartedly believe that each one of us is unique and in that uniqueness, perfect. But it's strange how we often have to relearn the same lesson. Life gives us a chance to reaffirm our beliefs by challenging them. I learned this lesson for the first time when I wrote my chapter in *Passionistas: Tips, Tales, and Tweetables*. It was agonizing to write, but when I submitted my chapter, I felt a catharsis and thought I had learned my lesson: Be my authentic self. Done. It turns out once wasn't enough. In fact, we have to keep slaying the demons of doubt against our own brilliance. Again and again they rise. Eventually, we will get so good at slaying that they will lay in the grave.

I write to share this lesson with other people. I write blog posts and chapters and letters and whole books because I want to help people feel less alone. I write to show you that us being different is what makes us the embodiment of the infinite complexity and love of the universe, or as some like to call it, the image of God. When I have the honor of editing someone else's words, I edit to celebrate their unique essence. I want their true words and meaning to shine through so that they can reach the people who are a part of their tribe.

To those of you who, like me, have spent years obsessing about fitting in and being who you're "supposed to," I leave you with a nugget of wisdom that I fell in love with while writing this chapter. *Different is better than good.* Stop worrying about whatever, and accept that you are meant to stand out. Give yourself permission to love yourself for who you are. Other people WILL love you for the true you too.

TWEETABLE

I am as __(your adjective here)___ as I am. And that is enough.

Takara Sights is a #1 Amazon best-selling author, editor, and speaker. In addition to this book, she has edited inspirational powerhouses including Passionistas with Erika De La Cruz, Little Black Book of Fitness with Jeanette Ortega, and Mom & Dadpreneurs with Kelli Calabrese in partnership with publisher and legendary marketer Kyle Wilson. Her clients and friends know her as an open-hearted, chill, and ambitious thought leader and explorer of knowledge.

*Check out more of her work at
takarasights.com
@takarasights
Snap: takeezi*

CHAPTER 21

Heroes Among Us –
Honoring Family Veterans

by Tim Cole

One man's trash, another man's treasure.

My plan was simple. Sort through moving and storage boxes cluttering our garage; glean important legal/financial documents and family keepsakes; then properly dispose of everything else. The process was derailed when I opened several boxes labeled "Veterans." Each box held dozens of manila file folders I'd previously labeled with the veteran's name containing the tangible record of my research efforts helping their family or friend honor their military service. My passion is honoring our military veterans. Today, I serve the loved ones of veterans living or deceased, doing extensive research on their veteran's military service, compiling the information within historical context to help them and other civilian, non-military families understand the significance of their military service accomplishments. When possible, I present these findings by sharing the veteran's story in a recognition ceremony.

Prior to my storage box rediscovery, if asked about my experience honoring veterans, my best guess was a couple dozen veteran honoring efforts throughout the last 15 years. The reality rediscovered in the boxes was surprisingly closer to a couple hundred veteran honoring efforts.

These began 25 years ago with my efforts to learn more about our family's military service and to recognize honorable service and sacrifice in a memorable way. Here is how our family story begins:

"Who is that?" I asked respectfully, pointing to the portrait of a handsome, uniformed soldier prominently displayed in great-grandmother's front room.

"That's James, my son, he was killed in the war." was her solemn, sad reply. As a young grade-schooler, I was surprised to hear my own name. James was MY name! I knew it was my father's name as well. Who was this other, mysterious James Cole in the portrait? I eventually learned Dad was named for his father's younger brother James long before "the war," World War II, had ever begun. Today, I have a handful of vivid memories of childhood conversations with Great-grandmother Cole. I've never forgotten that day first learning about Uncle James, the sharp-looking, beloved soldier memorialized in the portrait.

Thirty years later, I honored my father's military service at a family gathering. I presented Dad a framed shadowbox displaying his military medals, ribbons, and badges earned as a drafted soldier during the Korean War. I explained each award item to our family, who like many others today, are genuinely unfamiliar with the symbols of military recognition and the honor associated with each. Dad's emotional reaction reflected through misty-eyed tears of pride. We learned Dad was deeply proud of his military service, more than he'd ever shared in our lifetime of conversations.

From that experience, the vivid memory of the soldier's portrait from childhood came to me in a profound way! I wanted to know more about that man, the American soldier who died in World War II (WWII) and for whom my father and I were named. I began a quest to learn as much as I could about Uncle James, his life before and during WWII military service, as well as eventually the combat circumstances of his death. Through family conversations and genealogical information, from conversations with his military buddies who served and survived WWII, and from research through the National Archives, I began to learn about a heroic U.S. Army soldier Private First Class (PFC) James Cole I never knew, nor had heard spoken of so openly and fondly.

PFC Cole was awarded the Bronze Star Medal and Purple Heart for his heroic combat service and ultimate sacrifice, along with other military awards. He was respected and well-liked by his fellow soldiers. My aunt provided a copy of the personal letter sent home to my grieving great-grandmother just after her son James gave his life in the defense of our nation.

The letter reads:

> *February 8, 1945,*
>
> *Somewhere in the Philippines*
>
> *Mother Cole:*
>
> *This is the most difficult letter I ever attempted to write. Words to express my true feelings are not at my disposal, so I will do the best with what I have.*
>
> *It may ease the pain in your heart to know that the Good Lord didn't let Jimmie suffer too long. For myself and on behalf of the entire*

Company, we want you to know that Jim's absence is a great loss to us. He was of the same disposition week in and week out and he was more fun than a good show.

Jim's last thoughts were of you for I was beside him when they carried him away. He hoped you all wouldn't take it too hard for he disliked hurting you.

If there is anything I can do or you would like to know please don't hesitate to ask me for it would be a joy to help in any way possible.

The Company and the fellows of James' platoon, including myself, know that we have lost a very good friend and someday we'll meet him in Soldier's Heaven.

In closing I would like to pass this verse along to you. It is found in the Book of John, 5th Chapter, 24th Verse: "Verily, verily I say unto you, he that heareth my word and believeth on him that sent me hath everlasting life and shall not come into condemnation but is passed from death to life."

Sympathetically yours,

Sgt. Winford A. Evans and the men of Company K.

Wink and a prayer.
Despite the many decades since its origin, Sergeant Evans' solemn, sincere letter to my great-grandmother captured my heart the moment I read it. I was determined to find Sergeant Evans to thank him on behalf of our family for his personal kindness, care, and concern.

By the war's end in August 1945 over 16 million Americans served in military uniform, at a time when our nation's entire population was just 135 million. Over 400,000 Americans lost their lives defending our nation, our American freedoms, and our individual liberties. The military began returning the earthly remains of our fallen military to their families who requested a stateside burial. My aunts shared that a Mr. Evans not only attended the local funeral held for James Cole in February 1949, he consoled my great-grandmother and shared stories of his valued friendship with her son. My aunts' post-war memories contradicted that of my more recent conversations with war buddies from the 1st Infantry Regiment who believed "Wink" Evans (as he was known) died of combat wounds received in a fierce battle near the very end of the war. Despite this disparity, I was driven to find Mr. Evans, thank him personally for his devotion and care to our family at a time of great loss, and learn more about his military buddy and good friend, my Uncle James.

The journey to find Mr. Evans and his family took many turns. Some good news was that, exactly as my aunts had recalled, Mr. Evans indeed survived the war, recovered from his combat wounds received in battle, and attended the stateside funeral of his buddy James Cole. I learned that after the war, back home in Missouri, Wink Evans married and began a family. Like so many veterans of what Tom Brokaw described as the Greatest Generation, also known as the Silent Generation, Mr. Evans never spoke about the war with his family. Wink Evans did not join his combat unit's member association, nor did he contact other wartime buddies. Still, I found a paper trail.

In the decades after WWII, Wink Evans moved his family to Iowa, found factory work in a foundry there, experienced divorce, remarried after many years, and eventually retired from the foundry company. With disappointment, I learned from a small-town newspaper that Mr. Winford A. "Wink" Evans passed away in Iowa in 1991 at the age of 73. He was buried in nearby Rock Island National Cemetery. Aware of Mr. Evans passing, I redirected my desire to share our family's gratitude for Mr. Evans to his family, an adult daughter living in a community near my own extended family. At this time a discovery was made, something rare and usual, yet divinely amazing!

One year later, I was honored to stand alongside a United States Army Lieutenant General (three-star) as the late Staff Sergeant (SSG) Winford A. Evans' was awarded the Army's Distinguished Service Cross for his individual courage and valor under fire in those final days of the war in the Pacific. The Distinguished Service Cross (DSC), our nation's second highest award for valor surpassed only by the Medal of Honor, was belatedly presented to his daughter on behalf of SSG Evans along with his many other decorations for valor and combat service throughout WWII.

Just as his military buddies had shared with me, SSG Evans was engaged in a fierce battle in the final days of the war which resulted in his medical evacuation due to the seriousness of his combat wounds. Wink Evans' valor under fire in that violent battle prompted unit leaders to nominate him for the Distinguished Service Cross. SSG Evans' DSC award was approved by HQ Army in December 1945 (three months after the war's end).

At the time SSG Evans was under medical care at locations overseas and then here in the United States. His combat unit, 1st Infantry Regiment, departed the Philippines and was assigned post-war occupation duties in Korea while our nation's military services were busy discharging over 50,000 service members each day. Regrettably, in his lifetime Wink Evans never knew he was awarded the Distinguished Service Cross.

Five decades later, on a special day of ceremony and recognition, the Cole and Evans families, were able to meet and share thanks for the mutual friendship, service, and sacrifice of our families, one for another. We were honored that the award ceremony was attended by many of Wink Evans' and James Cole's surviving war buddies from their WWII combat unit, along with a host of current military service members. Later that year, SSG Winford Evans' heroism was read into the U. S. Congressional Record. Today, at Rock Island National Cemetery SSG Winford A. Evan's gravestone recognizes his personal valor and heroism during World War II, listing his significant combat decorations, including the Distinguished Service Cross.

Treasure!

As I completed my storage box rediscovery, I was powerfully reminded of the breadth and depth of these honor-filled endeavors: from simple efforts helping request, research, and translate military records to preparing and hosting full ceremony-like veteran honoring celebrations around the nation, some covered by news media. I've been blessed by reminders of valued relationships, the expanse of past efforts and events at locations across our nation, across multiple generations, and across all branches of service, from World War I to our present global war against terrorism. Within these boxes and recaptured from faded memory, was loving correspondence of gratitude and thanks, and even upbeat photos and news stories that captured each day. Many efforts were on behalf of our Greatest Generation WWII veterans, and it is not lost on me that many have passed since our collaboration.

Today, I am inspired, motivated, and devoted to continue my calling to help others honor their patriot's legacy, to edify, uplift, and encourage... to bring honor, hope, and healing to veterans and their families. I've been doing just that for more years than I had recalled. With gratitude and joy I reflect back, reminded of these heroes, their loving families and their growing, lasting legacy. Today, I continue this personal mission, this calling to help families learn about, recognize, and honor their beloved military veterans, bringing honor and healing to all involved.

Freedom is not free.

For so many of us Americans freedom has been given as a great gift. Our unique American freedoms, our individual liberties, and our vast economic and educational opportunities have been purchased at great cost through the service and sacrifice of generations of past military veterans and these uniquely American blessings continue to be defended today by our current generation of military service members.

Value freedom. Honor a loved one's military service. Recognize their sacrifice! Freedom is not free.

TWEETABLE

Honor your family's military service legacy. You CAN bring honor, hope and healing to your veteran & our veteran families. It is a treasure!

31-year "Mustang" Marine Corps Colonel Tim Cole honors military veterans via their loved ones. He expertly guides family/friends of beloved veterans (living or deceased) through a process of research, evaluation, historical context, and recognition, honoring their veteran's military service. Families share the impactful legacy such recognition generates along with honor and healing.

Who is your beloved veteran to be honored?

Email: tim@coloneltimcole.com
Webpage: www.coloneltimcole.com

CHAPTER 22

Getting Fired While Pregnant
The Greatest Gift I Ever Received
by Monick Halm

shook my head slightly and hugged my belly. Had I heard what I thought I heard?

My boss was staring at me from across his desk. "Tomorrow is your last day." He glanced down briefly at my belly. "I'm sorry."

Two weeks ago I had been lamenting the fact that I was five months pregnant and I still didn't look pregnant. I just looked like I'd been gaining weight. My sister-in-law who had gotten pregnant within two weeks of me, had a perfect "baby bump" at three months.

Five days earlier I rejoiced when my bump finally started to show. I'd gone maternity clothes shopping, and my closet had a new set of clothes "perfect for the office."

Now, I had just been fired. I was five and a half months pregnant and I looked it. How was I going to find another job now? Who would hire a very pregnant woman?

I stared at my boss as he talked about the logistics of my leaving my job. He concluded with "Any questions?"

I blinked back the tears and shook my head. I quickly ran back to my office and closed the door. I couldn't believe what had just happened. I felt like I'd been punched in the gut—my very pregnant gut.

After a recent court victory and some stressful 100+ hour weeks, I was expecting to receive a hefty bonus, not my walking papers!

That night I lay in bed staring at the ceiling. My wise husband gave me space to think as he made dinner. I was still in shock and disbelief. My mind was racing. I was trying desperately to think of how I could find another law job at this point. Tears of frustration and fear were streaming down my cheeks and onto the pillow. All I could think of was "who is going to hire me now? What am I going to do?"

Growing up I'd been taught that the key to a successful life was to do well in school, get a professional degree, become a lawyer, doctor, engineer, or professor, and live happily ever after. That was the formula. That was the path. That was the safe and prudent thing to do.

I'd always been a "good girl" and a rule follower, so I did what I was taught. I was an A student, I got a Columbia Law School education, became a lawyer, and was working hard, making a nice six-figure salary at a boutique intellectual property law firm.

As for the "happily ever after" part? I'd been working as a lawyer for nine years at that point—and I'd vacillated from feeling "somewhat unhappy" to "desperately miserable" the whole time. On a scale of 1–10 (1 being "please just kill me now" and 10 being "ecstatically blissful"), my law jobs had ranged from a 2–5. On a very good, very rare day, it could be a 6.

This particular job had been "somewhat unhappy" (4-5) so I figured I'd stay put. My paycheck was needed at home. And even though I worked until well past midnight on most days, and didn't enjoy the majority of my work, it wasn't the worst job I'd ever had. My standards weren't very high, and you don't make drastic changes when you're pregnant, right? You take the safe path.

God had another plan for me though.

As I stared at that ceiling, a calm quiet came over me. A voice whispered to me *"Let it go. Receive the gift you have been given."*

"Gift?!" I whispered back to the voice. "How could this be a gift?"

Look and you will find it.

That voice told me to let go of finding another law job. I mentally agreed. It would be an uphill battle to find another job now anyway, so I would wait until at least after the baby was born and I'd had a short maternity period.

This voice also whispered, *"This is a moment to find something new."*

What if the story I'd been told about "get a good job as a lawyer or doctor, and you'll be happy and safe" wasn't true? It sure seemed to be a load of crock to me. What if I took this time to actually find something that would make me happy? What if I used this gestational period to birth something else new?

Life wasn't meant to be lived at a 2–5 (or 6 on a good day), was it? What if I could find something new that would be a 10?

That day was perhaps the most difficult in my life, but it gave me an opening. It forced something from my hands that I'd been holding on tightly to, even though that thing was mediocre at best. It gave me the space to fill it with something new, something better.

It was not a straight path, but getting fired, when I couldn't just hop back into another miserable job, opened the door.

A few months later, in August of 2008, I gave birth to my daughter.

A few months after that I started a coaching certification program. That coaching business slowly built, and I began to get more and more clients—these were women wanting to work with me around issues of career, money, and abundance. I loved the work I was doing and the impact I was able to have on my clients. Instead of being at a 4, my life started nearing an 8 or 9. A year after that my husband and I started flipping houses on the side. I'd spent years watching HGTV shows and thinking "that would be SO fun!" And then suddenly here I was doing it. And it was really fun!

It was an amazing feeling to take an ugly property and make it beautiful and more functional. We improved the property value on that house, sold it to a new owner who loved it, and increased the values in the entire neighborhood. We were leaving the property and community better than we found it.

We started flipping houses in LA after the bubble burst and home values were relatively inexpensive. We were able to make a good living doing this at first. After a while the margins were getting slimmer and slimmer and it was becoming harder and harder for us to find the right homes for profit. Also, we realized that after every flip, we had to start all over again. We wanted to buy and hold on to a property and generate passive income.

We started to look for a four-unit building in Los Angeles. It was 2015 and very expensive to find a property that would cash flow and made sense. I was very frustrated, and unsure about what to do.

It was through a connection in my mastermind group I was introduced to the perfect person that helped me take that next step.

I believe in the power of masterminds. Masterminds are a group of people who come together with a common purpose. In a mastermind you share ideas and resources to help your fellow mastermind members achieve their dreams and goals. I was in a mastermind at the time with five extraordinary business people, who are all exceptional at what they do. One of them was Kyle Wilson, Jim Rohn's 18-year business partner and president of Jim Rohn International.

Kyle introduced me to his 20-year friend, Robert Helms. Robert Helms is the host of the The Real Estate Guys™ Radio Show and podcast, the most popular real estate podcast in the world. In addition to being a radio show host, Robert Helms is a a real estate investor and developer with hundreds of millions dollars worth of real estate investing deals under his belt. He was someone I was thrilled to meet, and in one 10 minute conversation Robert completely changed everything for me.

In that ten minutes I realized where I'd been going wrong.

First, my husband and I were looking in an expensive property market where the numbers didn't make any sense for what we were trying to do. Robert told me "live where you want to live, invest where the numbers make sense." I hadn't thought of investing in a market outside of where I lived. I just assumed I had to be able to drive to the property and check it out. Hearing him say that literally opened up the world to us.

Second, we were not taking advantage of leverage. He opened my mind to the idea that instead of trying to get one four-plex by ourselves, we could partner with a group of investors and get a 100 or 200-unit building. We could have a much bigger payout with less work and less risk.

Third, I realized I wasn't around people who were thinking big enough. In my previous crowd, pretty much everyone thought getting a four-plex was a big deal. No one I knew would have conceived of investing in a 200-unit apartment building!

I decided right then and there, I wanted to be around folks who were thinking much bigger and to learn to think like them.

That night I went home and told my husband we were signing up for the next The Real Estate Guys™ syndication seminar. This process of partnering with investors to purchase properties is called "syndication," and I wanted to learn how to do it from someone who had been successfully doing it for decades. We signed up and bought our plane tickets to Phoenix that night.

We attended the Secrets of Successful Syndication Seminar in January of 2016. Since then we've attended many different real estate conferences all over the country and around the world. We've joined two real estate mentoring groups. We have watched dozens of hours of training videos and read half a dozen books.

I'm a constant learner anyway, and because I am dealing with large sums of other people's money it was important to me to make sure I knew what I was doing.

We have invested hundreds of hours and tens of thousands of dollars to learn how to successfully invest in real estate, and it has paid off.

What we've learned and the community we've surrounded ourselves with has really helped us collapse time frames.

This side gig turned into my main gig: real estate investor. Now instead of flipping single family houses, we started investing in apartment buildings and other larger properties in need of rehab and repositioning.

We are still working on leaving a property and community better than we found it, though now on a larger scale and over several years (versus several months that we would take for the single family homes). We are rehabbing apartments, improving management, removing certain "bad elements" living in the buildings, and overall making it a much nicer place to live for the tenants and the neighbors.

While we do this, we have investors that contribute money to buy the buildings with us. Syndication has become my favorite way of investing. For bringing the deal together, I am able to get some of the cash flow and equity. I'm able to invest using other people's money (OPM).

My investors are also able to leverage OPM. (They put in a little and are able to own a piece of a property that they would likely not have been able to purchase on their own). They also leverage OPT (other people's time). We "active syndicators" do all the work of finding the deal, vetting it, putting it together, and managing it. The passive syndicators just pay in once and collect checks as the properties cash flow and increase in value.

I love this type of work. There's a ripple effect of prosperity as we, our investors, the real estate brokers and agents, contractors, lawyers, accountants, local tradesmen and vendors, insurance brokers, lenders, sellers, and the local community all benefit from these transactions. It's win-win, and easy to leverage.

In less than two years we passively invested in a 320-unit apartment building in Dallas and a 454-unit apartment complex in Atlanta, syndicated a 109-unit mobile home park in North Carolina, a 77-unit apartment complex and a 51-unit apartment complex in Albuquerque and a 199-unit workforce housing project development in Louisiana, and are currently working on a ground-up development of a 240-unit apartment building in Louisiana.

And we're accomplishing all this for less money than we would have invested to buy that four-plex in Los Angeles.

I'm not sharing this to brag, but to show what is possible.

All this has been great. But...there was one big thing I noticed was largely missing from all the trainings I went to: the feminine presence.

I'd look around these rooms where I was learning incredibly valuable information and usually less than 10% of attendants were women!

There are relatively so few women in the real estate investment realm, and I desired to change that. That desire led me to create Real Estate Investor Goddesses.

Real Estate Investor Goddesses was born at that first seminar we went to in January 2016. The seminar took place on a Friday and Saturday. My husband and I stayed at the hotel through Sunday. That Sunday morning I went to the hotel gym and got on the elliptical.

As I pedaled back and forth, my mind processed the incredible two days I'd just had. I felt like I'd been let in on a huge secret about how to truly build wealth in the country… in a way that was so win-win and positive. Doing this right, you can build a life of financial and time freedom. It was perfect for me as a woman and mama.

But why were there so few women in that room? In a room of approximately 120 people, there were maybe 9 women in the room. We were less than 8% of the room!

I continued to pedal back and forth on the elliptical, and I thought of what one of the teachers, Russell Gray, kept saying. "You want to build your brand and build your network. Who do you want to work with?"

It all came to me as a stroke of insight. That voice told me that I was meant to work with women and real estate. It made so much sense—I wanted to work with women! I wanted to bring more women in that room. What I was meant to do came together as a perfect 10—marrying my love of coaching women around wealth and abundance with real estate investing. Real Estate Investor Goddesses was conceived. The business and the book I would come to write, *The Real Estate Investor Goddess Handbook*, were downloaded to me in one instant.

Over the next few months, I birthed a business helping women create passive income streams in real estate so they can build wealth, create the lifestyle they desire, and make the massive difference on the planet they came here to make. I know that when women have time and money they give back to their families, they give back to their communities, and they give back to the world.

Also, I know many women don't have the time and energy to dedicate to learning and managing real estate like I do. I love showing women how they can invest in real estate passively and enjoy the passive income streams and great tax benefits without having to deal with tenants, toilets, and termites. I am thrilled to have been able to help hundreds of women so far to do this.

I am so grateful to be doing work that I love and that is truly life changing.

When I think back to that moment in 2008 when I sat across from my ex-boss as he told me that I was fired from a job that represented not only my livelihood but also my identity as a lawyer, it felt like my life came crashing down around me. I was in such grief at first. I felt sorrow, that turned to anger, and finally acceptance.

Now I'm just filled with gratitude. I am grateful for that kick out of my "comfort zone." It allowed me to birth a new business, a new life, and a blissful new me.

TWEETABLE

Be grateful for getting kicked out of your "comfort zone." This gives you the space to create something new—something better.

Monick Halm is a #1 best-selling author, podcast host, founder of the Real Estate Investor Goddesses women's investor community, real estate coach and mentor, and real estate developer, syndicator, and investor with over 1100 rental doors. She can be reached at @MonickPaulHalm on twitter, on the Real Estate Investor Goddesses Facebook Page, or at www.RealEstateInvestorGoddesses.com

CHAPTER 23

Dreams on Trial
How to Win Over the Silent Jury Within that Keeps Us Stuck

by Sean Murphy

It has been a 50 year journey. The moments when I felt I was not in control of the events in my life have been many. I remember at age five when I thought the world had ended because one of my dogs was hit by a car in front of the house. I remember the time I was 14 and my family was shattered with a story of what seemed like tragedy. How was I able to get through these moments? What helped you or hurt you?

Fast forward to 2004. I'm married to my bride with an eight month old. Our home, our dream home, was destroyed by three different hurricanes within weeks of each other. How much can you take? The answer is a lot.

I finally was given the "corpus," the blueprint, I needed to understand how we make it out of the depths of despair. Others never do. After all my training, I was shocked that it was a four day jury trial that I was picked to sit on that revealed to me not only a book that is in the works, but also countless new trainings and keynotes I've already given to my corporate clients as well as my personal students. It gave me the words, the wisdom, to help 1000s of people around the globe see in a clear and precise fashion what I had been trying for 30 years to explain. It's good, I promise!

So let me share with you an insight into this new understanding that being a juror revealed to me.

We are, every one of us, doing our best to live up to the expectations of other people. It is called approval addiction. Unless you know the simple, easy way to recognize it, develop a plan for it, then execute it, the next goal you set will be like so many others, just a wish!

For over 30 years I've studied the human brain and why it does what it does, and I have to say, until recently, we were all looking at success in a "losing" way! Seriously! Let me see if I can give you some great content in this short story. Are you ready?

Have you not asked someone out or not asked someone for help because of the answer you might get from them? We fool ourselves into thinking avoiding fear is being successful, it's not. That's the fear of rejection. I bet you are like me, and you are addicted to avoiding rejection right? You can't argue that; at least 99.9% of the population wants to avoid it. These are addictions that were wired into us from our childhood. We have become so used to these addictions. We call that a functional addiction.

Wait, it gets even more interesting.

Have you ever set a goal and missed the target date or, maybe even worse, told yourself that it's not important anymore? Even more tragic is, we forget about the goal all together.

That is the addiction to sameness.

Now before you get all mad at me or even argumentative, let me get very blunt with you. Have you ever avoided something because of how it was going to make you feel? Knowing full well that if you achieved the request, the ask, the goal, your life could dramatically improve? I would imagine you have to say yes to that! I know I do.

It's why I want to share with you some profound, simple steps you can take to begin to take back control of who you really are.

The killer is dopamine!

Do me a favor, ask yourself, when you hear a sound, see a picture, taste some food, or smell something, how much of what you are doing, is making it INTO the brain? I know, crazy question, but I want you to think about it. So, understand that everything that happens to us, everything that we remember or experience, is happening at a chemical level. You get that right?

So if all our interactions and memories and thoughts are some form of chemical cocktail, then we should know the ingredients for success and the ingredients for failure, right? I mean, after all, we have been studying the secrets of success for hundreds of years, we should at least have a basic ingredient list right? Wrong.

Our cocktail for success is rarely ever created by ourselves, it's been the opinion of others. I call them the jury of our mind!

Think for just a moment, do you have a habit that one of your parents has or grandparents have? Has anyone ever said, you remind them of someone in your family? "OMG, that's just like your Uncle Henry...."

We have on average 70,000+ (more than seventy thousand) thoughts a day! Science reveals to us that about 90% of those thoughts are repetitive! That means that the goals you are setting today to overcome, to change, to grow yourself have to compete with years of previous thoughts and conditions that have made you who you are. Dr. Dispenza says, "Your personal reality, makes up your personality."

Okay Sean, if this is even the slightest bit true, how the hell am I ever going to compete against all the opinions of the thoughts I have running in my brain!

Easy! You have to become aware!

The first thing they tell any addict is that they need to be at a point in their life that they ask for the help, that they agree with themselves that this is no longer the way they want their life to go.

Are you there yet?

If you are, here is what to do next.

It comes down to a simple math equation! Let me ask you, if you were going into a fight, and there were four or five of them, and just one of you, could you win?

Absolutely, you would say. If the thing I was fighting for was worth it, I could stop anyone! I would agree! The reality is, if that was the case, it would have to be life threatening, wouldn't it?

So why then would we let any goal be lost? After all, isn't the END GAME OF LIFE death?

It comes back to a math problem about the six areas of influence. This is how you beat that jury of your mind which delivers the verdict on your wants and dreams the instant you set a goal to be different or to have more or do more! If the verdict is guilty...you can't do it, and you are imprisoned where you are!

How old are you right now? Is this where you said you were going to be 10 years ago or even two years ago? So you are pretty much the same; you've had some incremental growth maybe. Is that why you woke up this morning? For incremental growth?

Here is the math problem explained.

If you are not aware of the six social influences that can affect you, you wind up stuck where you are, because few have been taught them.

All too often, we focus, if you can call it that, on maybe two of these, and they are both in the motivation column.

When you have someone sit you down and create a road map that deals with ALL six of these, your results are increased 10X in success, and this is based on proven research.

You are capable of great things, you know that. You feel that in every cell of your body! What keeps you up at night is wondering why the world seems to be conspiring against you!

It's not! It's that damn jury of your mind, the silent jury that seems to say nothing, just like in a courtroom, yet delivers the knockout punch at the very end of any trial. They only do one thing, pronounce Guilty or Not Guilty!

So, question, have you been guilty of not reaching your goals, not achieving the targets you promised others? Now you know it's a simple math problem, and it is time to change the way you play the game called goal setting.

It is time for you to have the leverage you need, the leverage you want, and silence the jury that has been keeping you stuck for so long.

Well, in my book, I teach you how to take back your life, how to put the math problem of influence back into the winning column.

1. **Personal Motivation** – What's keeping your motivation low? It is stress, a poor relationship, your job that's not going so well? These challenges can keep you from "getting motivated."

2. **Personal Ability** – "The Jury" – You have the ability to change what you need to in order to get started right now. Recognize the thoughts you have when you say, "I'm going to, I have the ability to get started." If you fail to start, it is most likely the jury of past programing stopping you.

	Motivation	Ability
Personal	1. Personal Motivation	2. Personal Ability
Social	3. Social Motivation	4. Social Ability
Structural	5. Structural Motivation	6. Structural Ability

3. **Social Motivation** – What groups and activities are keeping you stuck? You know what I'm talking about. What groups could you get into that would help move you towards your goals?

4. **Social Ability** – There are groups that would be of great help for you, be it Facebook groups, or Meetups. Find someplace to harness your personal motivation and move it forward.

5. **Structural Motivation** – This includes current habits you have, what you do, and how you are programmed to deal with your environment. Do you go to the same bar after work on Tuesdays? What environmental patterns do you have that your "jury" keeps you going to?

6. **Structural Ability** – What about your environment can you improve for your benefit? That means the people you hang out with, the online chat groups you frequent, or the cable news channels you yell at because you get mad at the stories!

TWEETABLE

Approval Addiction will continue to cost us our life's work until we learn how to deal with it. Six steps to silencing the silent jury within.

For over 30 years Sean has been at the forefront of personal accountability coaching and mentoring. His clients include CEOs who want him to maximize their mindset as well as Mom & Dadpreneurs who want to leverage every drop of talent from their soul to be the best providers for their families.

To learn more about Sean's book, please visit www.seangmurphy.com for the companion information to this chapter, please visit addiction. seangmurphy.com for handouts and videos to help you on this topic.

2x Best-selling Author
Founder & CEO of Mental Profits
Husband and Dad

CHAPTER 24

How to *BE IN THE TOP 1%*, Going From Agent to Investor

by Bob Helms

What does "being in the top 1%" of real estate agents mean? It means you can be earning a six-figure income and creating an exceptional lifestyle for yourself. This is absolutely doable if you are serious about wanting to succeed. All you need to do is learn to "speak income" and then simply focus on helping investors find what they need to succeed.

So, why would I write a book to help real estate agents and investors become richer? Aren't they already rich? Well, here are a couple of things you probably don't know about them:

1. The average real estate agent in America earns $35,000 – $40,000 per year!

2. That agent usually doesn't understand income properties and doesn't own any themselves. They are clueless about how to assist real estate investors.

3. This means that real estate investors are desperate to find qualified agents to help them with their transactions…but, alas…there are almost none to be found who can actually help them. And that means that investors mostly have to fend for themselves.

4. Most real estate agents have no idea what an investment property specialist (IPS) is or that they have the opportunity to become a very successful IPS by focusing on serving investors. It will require some study and some coaching, but these tools are readily available, and the subject matter is not that difficult to learn!

5. Not only can real estate agents jumpstart their business by assisting investors, they can help the investors begin or increase their portfolio holdings dramatically by actively providing the professional services those investors are searching for. Investors who are just getting started will definitely need the most assistance and guidance, but all of them can benefit from your assistance.

When real estate agents are taught to focus on serving investors, two remarkable things happen. First, they quickly realize that there are virtually NO LIMITATIONS on the amount of business they can generate from commissioned sales in the investment property specialist niche. And, more importantly, they can now learn how to BECOME investors themselves, which will allow them to build a significant property portfolio to provide handsomely for their own lifestyle and their retirement! Becoming an experienced investor themselves will demonstrate an IPS's credibility and will attract other investors who will want to become their clients. Focusing on serving investors means you are dealing with clients who own multiple properties and therefore complete many more transactions each year. You continue to establish and confirm your value to those investors with each transaction you help them complete!

Happily, experienced agents don't have to abandon their owner-occupied residential buyers and sellers to participate in the investment property segment. My son Robert and I were a father and son real estate team for 18 years in Silicon Valley, and our transactions included approximately 35-40% income properties and 60-65% residential properties over that time period.

We had an advantage over most agents because we had been investing in real estate for several years and therefore could not only understand the investment picture, but also had ownership experience that provided credibility with clients and with other investment property specialists. Our personal investments included single family homes, duplexes, fourplexes, several small apartment buildings, a 50-unit apartment building, a medical-dental building, and a warehouse. In short, we already had an investor mentality and properties that provided our experience credentials, enabling us to give sound advice to clients.

BE IN THE TOP 1% emphasizes the importance of learning how investment real estate is done early in your career and starting to invest as quickly as you can. This allows you to start achieving results as soon as possible while building your reputation as an experienced investor and advisor to your clients. It's not necessary to start out as an investor to become a successful IPS, it's just an advantage. You can definitely begin without any experience as an investor and build your portfolio of properties over time.

BE IN THE TOP 1% is ideally suited for real estate agents who want to learn to become investment property specialists because investors desperately need your help, and you can quickly become their go-to agent and valued team member! It's easier than you think, and the lack of trained IPS agents means you will have very little competition from other agents!

Let's identify the particular market segment that is readily available to these IPS agents and why it affords so much opportunity for them. The overall real estate marketplace is normally divided between residential and commercial properties, and both segments are handled by licensed real estate brokers and agents who concentrate on the practices peculiar to their area of specialization.

Residential brokerages normally assist their buyers and sellers with the sale or purchase of their personally owned-and-occupied single family homes—their residences. Although apartment buildings are also personal residences for their tenants, transactions involving these properties are handled by either commercial brokerages or by firms specializing in apartments.

Commercial property transactions for office space, commercial retail shopping, warehousing, and industrial properties are handled by commercial brokerages, including both leasing and sales activities. Although commercial agents may handle larger multifamily residential properties, they do not sell houses or smaller apartment buildings. Nor do residential agents often sell commercial properties, primarily because they don't have the necessary training and skills to handle those properties. (Commercial agents often receive the CCIM certification, recognizing them as certified experts in the commercial and investment real estate industry).

As you may anticipate, there is overlap between these disciplines. This often provides the opportunity for residential agents to participate in transactions involving commercial properties, particularly with properties that are small enough to be below a commercial agent's radar, meaning they are priced below his threshold of interest and are likely too small to attract his attention. So there is a sizeable portion of the market for many types of properties—probably those priced below $10,000,000 currently—which is often available to non-commercial agents on a case-by-case basis if you have the training, skills, and experience to participate. Most of what you will need to learn to take part in these transactions is presented in *BE IN THE TOP 1%*.

The complete title of the new book is, *BE IN THE TOP 1%—A Real Estate Agent's Guide to Getting RICH in the Investment Property Niche*, and in the book I share:

1. Why there is an opportunity right now for you to become a uniquely successful IPS and TRIPLE your income. Both new and experienced agents are capable of earning six-figure incomes when they learn how to "speak income" and focus on serving investors.

2. How to understand real estate investment properties and formulate a plan to become a successful investor yourself, while serving your investor clients and building your business.

3. How to correctly value income properties based on the income they produce.

4. How to understand the tax benefits of owning real estate. Your government wants you to be an investor and rewards you for providing housing and commercial rentals to others. These tax benefits essentially allow you to keep much more of what you earn from your rental properties.

5. How you can build and successfully manage a portfolio of investment properties that will create the lifestyle you want, while simultaneously providing for your retirement.

6. The factors you should consider when taking on partners to accelerate your business' growth. What are the reasons to consider partners and what are the precautions you should take before you engage them?

7. How you and your clients can use self-directed IRAs (SDIRAs) to invest in real estate, mortgages, and much more to obtain high returns, and how to learn the rules that apply.

8. How you can become a uniquely successful real estate agent by providing services other agents don't offer. Being the best is not an accident. The best agents include a plan to earn and retain their client's business, for life!

9. The habits of uniquely successful real estate agents that are designed to ensure that your clients will always want to use your services! Here we review winning techniques and strategies that have paid dividends for many years, and we emphasize not only what they are, but why they work!

In addition to teaching you the technical details you need to know about investment properties, this book zeros in on showing you how you can provide exceptional service to your investor clients. Delivering great service is not an accident. It must be your specific plan. Your clients will appreciate knowing that you value their business and that you will be available to assist them whenever you are needed. Great service will promote longevity in your relationships.

So, now that you know about this opportunity for you to excel as a real estate agent specializing in investment properties, the question is, "Does it excite YOU?" Can you see yourself as a top performing investment property specialist building both a new clientele of investors and your own income property portfolio? Because you will encounter very few IPSs who can compete with you to serve these investors, YOU are in control of your destiny! You can be as successful in this arena as you choose to be…Are you ready to *BE IN THE TOP 1%*?

TWEETABLE

BE IN THE TOP 1% teaches real estate agents to 3X their income, create a great lifestyle, and build a retirement all by serving investors!

What do you call a man who has been investing in real estate since 1957, a practicing real estate broker since 1980, and a mentor to Robert Helms, Russell Gray, and hundreds of others? We call him The Godfather of Real Estate. Most know him as Bob Helms.

Bob has probably forgotten more about real estate than most people ever know. Bob's wealth of experience makes him a featured contributor to The Real Estate Guys™ radio and TV shows and a popular speaker at live events.

To purchase Bob's book, BE IN THE TOP 1%, *or to utilize Bob's individual or group coaching, email bob@realestateguysradio.com.*

CHAPTER 25

Universal Kool-Aid

by Carmen Studer

The smart-ass little kid in me wanted to submit a short letter as my chapter and title it BE FREE LIKE ME.

Dear Beautiful Human,

Few people would pass up the unbelievable, once in a lifetime chance to write a chapter in a book project with the great Kyle Wilson, share their unique message with the world, co-create with these magnificent thought leaders, and get their name splashed in a most divine way. I did though. I wanted to bring home an important message and share with you the rich freedom I have cultivated. I am not bound by man (the pressure of delivering something that doesn't come from my core to please others). Not time (deadlines). Not the fear of missing out (on social proof, people of influence, or money). It took me 18 months of straight up meditative intention, emotional content invention/practice, open-minded seeking, and a deep and true love of the honorable within me to make this happen. I have awakened. My favorite hobby is teaching people how to embody this FREE spirit. I am presently practicing what I preach. Join me.... Peace OUT! Headed to watch fireworks at a private party.

Love,

Carmen Studer
aka Dragonfly!

Only someone living beyond her primitive and reptilian (fear based) brain could write the above letter. As the thoughts formed in my mind I thought, Damn...I really think that sums up my greatest message. That is fully applying my universal truths without seeking validation from outside myself. It is my belief that it is time for everyone to step up and embody their ideal self (their soul). This world is in desperate need of fearless and authentic leaders. This isn't about human measurement, goals, and grinding. This is the future of human ascension, manifestation, and creation. The smart ass in me is not all ass...She is part smart too. I will take advantage of this marvelous feeling inside me at this moment and the momentum this thought has created to write more than a letter. I will write my chapter. My soul approves, of course.

It is 7:30pm on deadline day, and I am just now starting my chapter after two failed attempts yesterday. What can I say; my highest self lured me away to do something more joyful. (The old me would have had this in early at any expense...not the new me... At one point I thought, *I wonder if my highest self will bring me into this collaborative project journey.* I am thankful she did.)

So, meet the new me...

Hello, my name is Dragonfly. God audibly gave me that name about 14 months ago, and I don't care if you doubt me. (The old me would have told some long story making sure you didn't think I was crazy because my sanity platform was more important than the person it represented). If you research dragonflies you will see how fitting it is for what I do and who I am. I encourage everyone to name and connect with his or her inner self. People name their cars, I think their souls should get at least that kind of respect.

I know my purpose(s). Well, we all have multiple purposes really. Think about this, even rocks have more than one purpose here on Earth. Yet when someone asks me my purpose my singular answer is to authentically embody my soul: the highest, wisest, most beautiful, richest, kindest, most honest, absolute badass, loving, super-natural self possible. (The old me didn't know I was sacred and worth cherishing before all others. I now know it is the only way to fully unlock all the gifts and inner guidance we are all endowed with upon birth.) My secondary purpose is to sell as many people as I can on the concept that their true desires are easily within reach simply by falling in love with inner/divine exploration. They have to meet their higher self, but also begin applying its leadings. We do this by stripping away as much dense and unwanted energy as possible. People are then free to actually experience an entire universe within. Even better...to become the master of the universe within.

I am a life coach. I am actually an aggressive sharer. I am gifted with the ability to see things from many perspectives (dragonflies have 360 degree vision). I can easily read the dominant energies a client is transmitting to the world. I have also created a system of very simple tools that allow people to purify who they are in order for them to step on to "Heaven on Earth." My tools seem trite and oversimplified at first...but they are highly potent. It is a system of infographics and worksheets that unveil hidden emotions and energies that weigh people down. I believe this will be the future of self-improvement. We are all capable of coaching ourselves with the right tools. Once you tap in, you begin to feel the awakening. I have coached a wide range of personalities, from youth out of prison to professionals: athletes, executives, business owners, and top actors. I have created a life where I sometimes get paid to take long walks around the lake with a client where I have the privilege of sharing the joy. Like a little girl with a universal Kool-Aid stand (and access to Skype).

I have deep spiritual roots. I have been very interested in the spiritual realm since my mom got cancer when I was 14 years old. I have made understanding the brain and spirit my number one hobby for nearly three decades. Her death was my unexpected gift; she became the wind beneath my spiritual wings. I was originally trained and permitted to teach *The Work* created by Byron Katie when I was 27 years old. I discovered Byron Katie five years or so before she ever appeared on *The Oprah Winfrey Show*. I love Byron's work. I watched her grow from rooms of 10 people to global guru on national television. It inspired me to create my own systems and tools. I look forward to the future unfolding. I can't wait to wake up everyday and live in the waves of possibilities.

I live what I teach. My gifts were always there, and I used them often in life, especially when mentoring youth from One Heart Project. One Heart Project is the 501(c)(3) charity I co-founded. I ended up on *Good Morning America* for my work on that project, but I didn't awaken to boldly claiming my gifts to the world until I hit my rock bottom after my divorce. This is where most people would tell their story that proves their character arc. I can't insert my story here because, as my own official life coach, I have sworn off heavy stories of the past unless needed for life saving purposes. I listen to every word a client says, and I am insistent about the benefits of removing negative words, phrases, and stories that don't serve our ultimate chosen destinies.

I believe deeply in the imagination (quantum creation). I created the new me through holographic rehearsals of the life I intended to embody. It trickled in at first, but more and more pours in daily. If you can imagine it, feel it, and believe it, you can and will have it.

My coolest trick is meditation. I can sustain the brain wave state necessary to elicit a frequency where I get "chills of truth" (the kind you get when you watch the Olympics) for hours at a time. Pure connection to source/God/intelligence where I receive "knowings," or "downloads," of pure joy, truth, clarity, and inspirations. I am 52 years old, I have traveled with billionaires, and nothing compares to the inner travel I have had alone and in meditation while connected to the divine. Have I sold you on meditation yet? I basically just told you one of my meditation sessions was cooler than a billionaire's yacht and private sea plane to a private island off the coast of Vancouver, Canada. And that is some of the most beautiful territory on

Earth. Once you can learn to tune yourself to this level of joy, you can be anywhere and feel like you are on vacation.

I live in Heaven on Earth. Yep, and I think it is the one Jesus was talking about when he said "on Earth as it is in Heaven." So you're probably wondering how it feels to be on this new version of Earth. I will give you a list of some of the visceral symptoms. I share this with clients as a progress checklist.

List of Healthy Spirit Symptoms / Activation Level 1 Checklist:
Love of Earth, animals, babies, children, adults of all colors and shapes. Love of your own body. People become transparent and easy to understand. Lack of feeling critical of self. Putting care of self first. Awareness of your own emotional triggers (good and bad). Knowing your purpose. Feeling amazing. Intolerance for feeling bad. Wanting to drink more water. Decreased interest in vices. Noticing signs, synchronicities, and symbols. Things becoming clear and confusion dissipating. Not needing to use your normal distractions. Lack of interest in television. Wanting to live unconditionally. Faith that all will be well. Goosebumps when you hear truths, witness greatness, or connect with the divine. Realizing when you judge others it is really about you. No interest in gossip at all. Refusing to blame others. Change in priorities. Increase in integrity. Hearing songs in the air. Desire to harmonize with others. Laughing easily. Patience coming naturally. Increase in trust in self. Increase in trust in God/Source/Universe/intelligent design. Seeing that clouds have pastel colors at the height of the day not just at sunrise and sunset. Enjoying time alone and with people. Looking into the eyes of your fellow man and finding something to love. Appreciation for geometric shapes. No feeling of being in bondage to anyone. Finding mundane things amazing (bubbles in a drink). Protectiveness of all humans. More openness to your sixth sense. Some dreams seeming real like an alternative timeline. Wanting to share the light with others. Becoming more interested in spiritual knowledge and wisdom. Believing no one needs pity, that everyone is capable of being sovereign. Inspiration to create. Smiling more. Strangers noticing your light. Enlightened people becoming drawn to you. Entertaining ideas you used to be closed to. Amplification of senses. Receiving job offers you aren't looking for. Ancient wisdom finding you. Asking for the best. Bigger thinking. Wanting to lift the hearts of others. Owning your quirks. Love of long walks. Fear not often being an issue. Walking away from drama. Faster healing. Getting sick less and less. Overwhelming joy staying for longer and longer. Feeling an addiction to positive. Tingling sensations during meditation. Sense of being supported by the unseen. Daily meditation. Disappearing of guilt and shame. Noticing patterns. Change in sleep patterns but you flow with it instead of resist. Careful placement of your energy. Daily journaling.

Unity, peace, and inner exploration becoming more interesting sometimes than outer. Abundance coming to you. Leading with love. Knowing your truth easily. Reading people better. Looking younger and more radiant. Making the best of any situation. Less panic. Change of friends. Willingness to say no. Inspiration to free yourself from restrictive patterns. And, following your intuition becomes commonplace.

How do you acquire these symptoms? Begin with radical self-care. Meet your sage within and begin trusting yourself, your universe, and your personal path. You can meditate/pray/listen quietly to the genius within. Or contact me...with the blessing of technology I have clients from Boston to LA. I always say, "Why study the masters when you can become one?"

You want to know why I consider myself a successful life coach? Two things happened. One, my 25-year-old son Dane came to me with a request to learn how to meditate, and two, my 20-year-old daughter Carlisle tells everyone we meet they need a life coach. I have never asked either of them to engage in what I do, I simply embody it. Heavenly living is highly contagious. There is nothing I want more than to connect with joy and witness it act as a lure for the desired creations in my life, except perhaps sharing this universal Kool-Aid with others. One taste of your magnificence within, and you will be hooked for life.

TWEETABLE

Stop studying the "masters" and become one. Upgrade your spirit. Perfect the science of YOU. Heaven on Earth awaits.

Carmen Studer, life coach, futurist, happiness expert, and lover of humans.

Carmen encourages people to get off the "Misery-Go-Round" and to begin INVERTING FEAR, STRESS, AND WORRY. Energy management is her specialty and she expects a lot from everyone's future! Every day offers great possibility. Stillness shouldn't just arrive in a vacation, it should be an expected part of the daily journey. To reach Carmen visit www.CarmenStuder.com.

CHAPTER 26

From Uncommon Mentors
My Lessons for Becoming Uncontainable
by Jim Gardner

I was a punk street kid who learned some hard, but valuable lessons on how to thrive by becoming uncontainable. Becoming uncontainable requires building systems of relentless, premeditated, meticulous rituals for elite performance. Now, as an elite performance coach, I teach elite athletes and leaders to become uncontainable and sought after in who they are and what they do.

Elite performance is the outcome of relentless daily improvements in preparation: spiritually, personally, and professionally. It's building a preparation legacy through physical, mental, and emotional fitness, value creation, leadership, connection, fun, and fulfillment.

If you're not thriving, you convince yourself you're doing well enough. Yet deep down you know you're making excuses and selling out on who you need to become. "What you don't think you can do is what we are going to do!" We will build your unique rigid adaptable systems of rituals and habits for becoming uncontainable.

This was the real message of the high school teacher that changed my life forever. He was paid to teach U.S. Government. However, Mr. Bourlard knew I needed a different system and by influencing me to do what I didn't think I could do, he saved the life of a troubled kid.

When my mom met Wes he was on the run, having escaped from prison in North Carolina. We lived in Kansas. Wes brought his life of cons and criminals into my mom's house and into my world. I never knew if or when someone would get shot, stabbed, or beaten during drunken card games and parties. It all happened. I slept most nights in my eight foot square room on a mattress on the floor with a knife in one hand and a steel pipe in the other.

Even amidst the racial unrest of riots and dusk to dawn curfews of 1968, I felt it safer running the streets than I did in my mom's house. I soon adopted the street life of crime. I became involved in the world of drugs, not as a user, but I was dealing everything from weed to narcotics.

My friends and I often blew things up or burned things down to get our prize. I didn't realize it at the time, but I was learning to develop relentless, premeditated, meticulous, rigid, yet adaptable systems, rituals, and habits of preparation. We surveilled a potential heist for days or weeks to find the safest patterns of opportunity. We knew the streets so well and planned so diligently, we would often taunt the cops for a little extra excitement. During nearly seven years running the streets, I never got caught. I never was arrested, not even close. As part of my system, and likely the most important lesson I learned on the streets, I listened with the intent of seeking to understand. Seeking to understand and respond often kept me out of harm's way. Those who reacted and couldn't control their attitude and actions suffered harsh and sometimes lethal consequences.

I began falling behind in junior high school because I couldn't read well, and found out years later I'm dyslexic. I felt I was street smart but book stupid, and no one around school had time for book stupid. I felt hopelessly trapped as an outlier in the assembly line of public education.

In high school my home world spiraled further down. Wes died of a heart attack. My mom then married a skid row alcoholic, followed by a no-account pothead making ceramics, and finally a railroader who made his real money in his side hustle using the railroad for interstate cocaine trafficking.

Somehow I survived to my senior year in high school, but was still hell-bent on the wrong side of the tracks. One day I was walking out of my U.S. Government class when Mr. Bourlard hollered out, "Gardner! Come back here!" Mr. Bourlard was a cynical hardass, but all the kids loved him. I walked back to his podium. He said, "Gardner, you're at a crossroad. I've heard the stories from the streets, and I've seen what you can do when you choose to attend school. You're either going to die soon, or you can change the world. Have you ever thought about going to college?" I laughed at him. I told him he knew what my grades were. And I told Mr. Boulard that on top of that, I hated school and the last thing I would ever do was more school. He had a different opinion.

Thanks to Mr. Bourlard influencing me to do what I didn't think I could do, I graduated with my senior class and started college the following September.

With a new vision for my life, I left the streets behind. Now, I needed to solve for how to fund college and my living expenses. No backsliding! I needed a legitimate job that paid decently. A friend since childhood had gone to work for McKesson, the pharmaceutical wholesaler. Oh the irony of delivering narcotics to local pharmacies. I was experienced and good at getting drugs to designated locations quickly. By making it a game for myself I continued to get faster at delivering and better at wowing my pharmacists. Consistently 75% faster than the other drivers, after a few short months I was promoted into the warehouse. I continued to build my systems of rituals, and by the time I was 21, I was running the McKesson warehouse, including the narcotics vault, and their IBM data center.

I had to choose an elective class to take at Wichita State. I thought, why not take a class on learning how to run legit businesses? Taking the handoff from Mr. Bourlard, my entrepreneurship professor, Ron Christy, took me under his wing.

Wichita, Kansas, my home town, has quite an interesting business history. It's the original home of Cessna Aircraft, Beech Aircraft, Lear Jet, Coleman outdoor products, Koch Industries, Rent-A-Center, and Pizza Hut.

Fran Jabara, former dean of the business school at Wichita State, consulted with several of the founders and leaders of these companies. Fran decided it would be helpful to the community and to the university for "business" to be better understood and to include the experience of the local resource pool. Tom Devlin, founder of Rent-A-Center, donated funding for a building on campus to house Fran's newly founded Center for Entrepreneurship where students would benefit from the experience of real-world successful entrepreneurs from right there in Wichita. Ron Christy, my professor, was named associate director of the center, and he soon asked me to get involved.

After I observed all that was going on at the Center for Entrepreneurship, I asked Fran if I could show him how it was possible to automate the business statements, forecasts, and proformas that were taking him and some of the others days to calculate manually. Fran was also a CPA, and I had never even taken an accounting class, but I could see a better system.

After my demonstration, I told Fran about a startup company named Apple that was building and selling microcomputers. Fran was so fascinated he threw me in his Mercedes and asked me to direct him to a guy I knew that sold the new Apple computers. Fran bought two Apple IIs that day with spreadsheet, database, and word processing software. He then hired me to come to his home on Saturday mornings to teach him and his high-school son Harvey how to use one of the Apples. A dyslexic street punk who mysteriously graduated high school was teaching a new system to a former business school dean and highly respected business consultant.

Throughout my journey I became very comfortable connecting with anyone. This enabled my most valuable lesson out of my Center for Entrepreneurship experience. I always surrounded myself with people who were out of my league. All of these people became my mentors by default, and I sought to serve them so I could continue to learn from them.

My grandpa, my first and greatest mentor, taught me the life sustaining systems to always "figure it out." He taught me to be independent by using creative thinking before asking for help.

From my professor, Ron Christy, I learned how to effectively manage multiple priorities during times of, what most would consider to be, chaos and crisis.

Fran Jabara, the creator of the Center for Entrepreneurship and the Apple computer convert, taught me how to negotiate anything and everything.

Frank Carney, co-founder of Pizza Hut, taught me to nurture relationships by always being authentic and he taught me the importance of timely and effective communication.

From Jack DeBoer, inventor of extended stay hotels beginning with Residence Inn, I learned the importance of self-awareness and objectively reviewing your failures and your successes, intentionally learning from both.

Tom Devlin, the founder of Rent-A-Center, was all about perseverance. When you get denied you don't ever let it stop you in business or on the basketball court.

The systems and rituals I learned from these mentors are what prepared me for leadership and executive positions that were in my future.

My journey with McKesson and the Center for Entrepreneurship opened the door to join a team at Pizza Hut that was developing a concept that we now know as point of sale. I began flying all over the southeastern United States to develop and test prototype devices and software from IBM, NCR, and others. Traveling over 50% of the time made it difficult to attend college classes. Finally, one of my professors told me I should leave college because the education I was getting in my work was a rare opportunity and that I could return to school in the future. Returning never happened, but I did get an extraordinary education that can't be taught in school.

Ron Christy, my entrepreneurship professor, watched what I was doing with retail process automation. He convinced me to leave Pizza Hut by giving me the keys to his multi-state furniture company so that, as general manager, I could develop and oversee the transformation to automated systems. I was realizing that when I worked relentlessly to make a difference by adding value, mentors noticed and opened doors I would have never been aware of.

I became obsessed with creating relationships with influencers and mentors so that I could continue to expand my knowledge and experience. Experience taught me that systems and organizations are only as good at the people supporting them. This began my passion for mentoring those around me as I continued to be mentored.

I read an article about a startup company in Dallas that was using computers and communication technology I was familiar with. I made contact even though, on paper, I was in no way qualified to work with these senior executives who had just departed computer services giant, Electronic Data Systems (EDS). While in Dallas for the annual furniture market I slipped off the radar long enough to have a conversation with Joe Glover, Naval Academy graduate, U.S. Marine, assistant to Ross Perot at EDS and now startup president.

Joe hired me into this group of mega achievers without me interviewing with any of them. Joe was more than a mentor, he became like a big brother and taught me everything he knew about business and instilled in me the grit to create extraordinary outcomes. Joe taught me to always spit shine my integrity.

New relationships and mentors continued to open new doors. Over the next 28 years, I had the fortunate opportunities to serve as a leader and executive for iconic brands including Tandy, L.D. Brinkman, Fidelity Investments, and Levi Strauss & Co.

As with my own unexplainable opportunities, my eleven-year-old daughter was invited to play in a junior golf tournament on spring break. She had played in the sandbox at the local driving range, but she never set foot on a golf course let alone play in competition. It was a cold, wet, miserable day for a kid's golf tournament. However to my amazement, my daughter loved it. I told her if she committed to learn properly, I would support her with lessons. The following weekend we ended up 35 miles from home at a place called Hank Haney Golf Ranch. That would become our home away from home for the next ten years. Hank and his coaches were teaching some of the top golfers in the world including Tiger Woods. My daughter became an elite junior golfer, earning a free ride through college. As a side benefit, dad received thousands of hours of observation and education in physical, mental, and emotional systems, rituals, and habits of preparation and for delivering extraordinary results.

Shortly after departing the corporate jungle I met John Maxwell, the leadership guru. I joined the John Maxwell Team as a founding member. My previous lid of awareness was shattered by the opportunities outside the corporate jungle and prevailing business models.

Loren Norris, a great friend I met through John Maxwell invited me to attend an entrepreneurial marketing event in LA: Craig Duswalt's RockStar Marketing BootCamp. I made it my mission to meet and develop friendships with Glenn Morshower, James Malinchak, Les Brown, Michelle Patterson, and others. In addition to friendships that developed, these people have mentored and coached me in the areas of acting, speaking, marketing, coaching, and entrepreneurship.

My ritual for intentionally expanding my relationships led to meeting and working with Bo Eason, a former NFL safety, playwright, actor, and coach. Bo has taught me how to live my story when I coach and speak.

I've worked with my friend Roger Love, the voice coach for speakers Tony Robbins, John Gray, Seth Mosley and musical artists John Mayer, Gwen Stefani, Def Leppard, and others. From Roger I've learned how to give my voice life and how to protect it as a speaker. Equally as important, Roger has taught me how the best voice coach in the world gives 100% focus and energy in every studio session.

Finally, through a National Speakers Association connection with Chris Widener, I met my current coach and great friend Kyle Wilson, founder of Jim Rohn International. Kyle is a marketing guru and his coaching has been significant in defining and positioning my services.

In reflection, I'm grateful for having survived the insanely dangerous environment I chose to participate in on the streets. I'm grateful Mr. Bourlard chose me and that his persistence changed my life forever, enabling all that followed that day in his classroom at the podium. And, I'm grateful my mom knows I've forgiven her.

My mission is to share all I've learned from my mentors, with all of my passion, with everyone that desires to become uncontainable and sought after for who they are and for what they do.

TWEETABLE

Becoming Uncontainable in who you are and for what you do with systems of relentless, premeditated, meticulous rituals, and habits.

Jim Gardner works with elite performers in sports and in business on **becoming uncontainable** *spiritually, personally, and professionally. Work with Jim today to build your Rigid Adaptable System for extraordinary outcomes while having fun and gaining fulfillment.*

Jim also has great passion for giving back in honor of those who gave of themselves in his life. He is blessed to periodically deliver the Monday morning devotional at Ziglar Headquarters. Jim speaks and mentors in high schools and for life-changing nonprofits including AdaptiveTrainingFoundation.org and BuildInternational.org.

JimGardnerLive.com
Jim@JimGardnerLive.com
JGardnerTX@Facebook.com
LinkedIn.com/in/JimGardnerLive
@JimGardnerLive

CHAPTER 27

From Borrowed Belief to No Limits

by Dan Sachkowsky

Life has an interesting way of letting us know what's possible. As a young boy raised in a poor home, there were definitely challenges which made me believe there were limits to what I could do. What others had, for example nice clothing, name brand sneakers, a nice family car, were all things that seemed to be so out of reach. At least that's what I was lead to believe until the day that I met the man who would forever change my life.

When I was 16 years old I met a man named Dave who was not only my first boss but who also became my life mentor. Dave was 30 years old. He came from a poor family as well, but he had a dream, and somebody told him he can accomplish anything that he wanted to do. At that time, like myself as a young boy, I loved what wealthy people had. I loved nice things, I just didn't know how it was possible to get them. Dave had a big successful business. He had three children, a beautiful family, a huge home, and an attitude of gratitude. Dave had a dream, and he set his sights high and had no limits. He became my idol. He was someone I always reached out to for advice. He changed my life by becoming my mentor and helping me believe that I could go above and beyond what I ever thought possible and live my dream.

This poor kid from a poor family who never had the understanding of how to become the successful businessman that he always dreamed of, used the belief of somebody else who believed in him more than he believed in himself to achieve everything he ever thought possible and more. This was possible because of Dave who was once a stranger that hired me to help him in his business. Little did he know, he would change my life forever and help me understand that life has no limits. It's amazing how one day you can go from having nothing to having so much success because of one person that believes in you.

20 years later I've done more in life and more business than I had ever thought was possible. I've met some amazing people in my circle of

influence, people just like me and also people who I just wanted to be around because they have accomplished big things and have big dreams. God puts people in your life to guide you, and it's up to you to utilize that direction and help put yourself in a place that you're always supposed to be in, a direction that you're always supposed to go.

I've had multiple businesses over the past 20 years and I've done many things which have all lead to the next big thing. Today I continue to dream big and strive for bigger things and I'll never forget who helped me understand that life has no limits. As you create business and success you meet some amazing people along the way and those amazing people help you meet more amazing people who become part of your future and point you in life's best directions.

The one thing I look forward to the most is becoming like Dave and believing in somebody more than they believe in themselves. Having somebody believe in you more than you believe in yourself is a powerful thing. It creates a bigger picture by expanding our vision of what is possible. Just because we are somewhere today doesn't mean we have to be there tomorrow. Over the years I have learned that no matter how high you get in life, you can always go higher. We all have a life with no limits. Our only limitations are the ones we put on ourselves because we lack the belief that we can achieve great things. Being an entrepreneur, business owner, speaker, and author, I can look back knowing these all were stepping stones to bigger things. But always remember, it all starts with desire—it is the starting point of all achievement. If you want to go somewhere, find someone who's already there and do what they're doing.

"When you have a dream it's there, it's tangible, it's really in front of you." When you have a dream, go after it. What's interesting is that people today may say or think it was easy for me to become a success because I'm already successful!

But the truth of the matter is, nothing is easy, and I attribute all my success to one thing. I never gave up and never made any excuses. I knew I could do it because Dave believed in me. Still to this day, I remember that conversation, and I will always replay it in my head when I want to set my mind on achieving bigger goals. When somebody else believes in you, it makes you unstoppable. Nothing binds you except your thoughts, nothing will limit you except your fear, and nothing controls you except your belief.

Always believe in yourself, because I believe in you, therefore you should believe in you.

TWEETABLE

Nothing binds you except your thoughts, nothing will limit you except your fear, and nothing controls you except your belief.

Dan Sachkowsky
Business leader, entrepreneur, speaker, author
Featured on NBC's Apprentice 2009 & 2011
Featured in Success magazine 2010, 2011, 2012
www.DanSachkowsky.com

CHAPTER 28

Millionaire Success Secrets:
How 7 & 8 Figure Entrepreneurs Think & Act Differently Than Others

by James Malinchak

Although today I am humbled to be one of the most requested and highest paid business and motivational speakers in America and have been featured on ABC TV's hit show *Secret Millionaire*, I didn't always experience the level of success that I'm blessed to have.

In my live event seminars, I always teach in a way that makes it easy for my audience to remember. When sharing with others, it's very important to keep things simple so people can easily comprehend your information.

There have been three major lessons that have absolutely changed my business and life and that I know can change yours, as well.

LESSON 1:
You Are NOT in the (fill-in-the-blank) Business!
You Are in the Business of Marketing Your Business!

I grew up in a small steel-mill town called Monessen, right outside Pittsburgh, Pennsylvania. There wasn't much optimism for life after the steeltown. Many never leave the town, which is totally fine. There's a specialness remaining in a town where you grew up. However, I had some big dreams and goals that I wanted to pursue, which would require me leaving our town in order to pursue them.

One day in junior high school, I was doubting myself and debating whether I could actually achieve my dreams and goals. Many thoughts of simply working in the mill after high school seemed to dominate my mind that day as my classmates and I were sitting in the school auditorium listening to a guest speaker.

The speaker shared a quote during his presentation that would forever change my life which was, "If you can dream it, you can do it. That means YOU CAN do anything you want to do in your life if you always believe in yourself and never listen to those who tell you that you can't do something!"

WOW! It was as though a lightning bolt of inspiration immediately shot through my spirit. Although I didn't know it then, that bolt of inspiration would go on to become a driving force in my life to this day that would allow me to achieve many of those big dreams and goals.

Fast forward. Eventually I left my hometown and went to play college basketball at the University of Cincinnati, before transferring and graduating from the University of Hawaii at Hilo.

After college, I noticed a deep desire beginning to surface. I began thinking, *Wouldn't it be cool if I could help people the way that speaker back in junior high helped me? Wouldn't it be amazing if I could speak words that would help others to change their lives, exactly how that speaker spoke words that changed my life?*

In that very moment, I decided to become a paid speaker who got paid for doing what he loved, changing people's lives!

There was only one big problem. I didn't know what the heck to do in order to become a speaker who actually gets paid so I began asking people who were speaking who gave the impression they were successful. Everybody I asked in the speaking industry, the "so-called experts" (a term I use lightly) all told me the same things: "All you have to do is dream big, have passion, tell your story and simply be a messenger."

Looking back now, I realized there are two problems with that advice: (1) Most who were telling me that (and most I find today) don't actually make any real money speaking; and (2) None of that advice matters if you don't know the business-side of speaking which is how you really get highly paid, or what I now teach others, how you become a Big Money Speaker®!

When listening to these "so-called experts" (a term I use lightly), I was literally financially broke and forced to work in a video store making $7 an hour to help support myself, while trying to figure out why I was a failure, not being able to make it as a highly paid speaker.

At one point, I lived in a tiny apartment that was so bad, there were actually steel bars on the windows to make sure nobody would break-in. I even slept every night with a softball bat just in case there was a break-in while I was sleeping (I'm not kidding).

Financially, it was getting tougher and tougher! Bills were coming in that I just couldn't cover. I tried everything to get paid and make money speaking, but NOTHING seemed to work.

Self-doubt continuously ran through my mind, while I constantly felt bad about myself that the reason I wasn't making it as a highly paid speaker was because I wasn't dreaming big enough, wasn't passionate enough, didn't want to help people enough, didn't want to make a big enough difference in the world.

I can't even begin to tell you how discouraged I became. There were SO many times when I thought about "throwing in the towel" and walking away from pursuing my dream of getting highly paid to speak for sharing my message. I seemed to be just "spinning my wheels" and often felt like a complete failure!

I had no idea what to do! I was about to fall flat on my face and give-up, when one day...**The Major Turning Point!**

I was talking on the phone with a mentor, who's very successful in business and a multi-millionaire. While we were catching-up on things, I asked him why most of his businesses were successful. I figured he would say something about his extensive business knowledge or 30+ years of experience. But his answer shocked me...and became the "KEY" that was the "turning point" for my entire speaking business! He said,

> *"The reason is simple and is what I actually consider to be the key for anyone to succeed in ANY business, even the speaking business! The reason is because you shouldn't study and learn from people in the industry because most don't know how to market to attract business. Study and learn from top MARKETERS!"*

> *"What? I'm not sure I follow you," I replied.*

> *He continued, "Nobody in ANY business could ever be successful if they don't know how to correctly market their products or services and get people to buy them. Just because someone is looked at as a top expert in your industry, doesn't mean they know how to market. So, why would you want to spend your time and possibly waste your money trying to study and learn from them? I'd rather just go right out and study and learn from top MARKETERS because they know how to do one thing better than anyone, MAKE MONEY FROM MARKETING!"*

WOW! Definitely NOT what I expected to hear! Immediately, a light bulb went off in my head! I knew this wealthy and successful mentor wouldn't have said that if he didn't mean it 100%.

What if I did the same!?! What if I studied and learned from top marketers and took what I learned and simply applied it to my speaking, writing, training, coaching and consulting business!?! Surely, it would work because principles are principles!

That was my aha moment. When I realized I'm not in the speaking business. I'm in the business of marketing my speaker services.

Realizing this and shifting my thinking instantly changed my business and life! I mean, instantly!

I went from where I was, "spinning my wheels," feeling like a complete failure, ready to give-up and quit, to becoming one of America's most requested, in-demand speakers delivering over 3,000 presentations, conducting over 1,000 consultations, authoring over 20 books and doing over 5,000 media appearances, including being invited by ABC TV to be featured on their hit TV show, Secret Millionaire.

In addition, years ago I created my Big Money Speaker® training teaching others how to become Big Money Speakers® sharing their message, story and how-to advice, helping tens of thousands of people from over 40 countries.

Even today in my Big Money Speaker® training, I begin the entire training by saying, "I believe you already have passion, mission and desire. You want to be a speaker because you want to make a difference in the lives of others. So we're not going to spend time discussing any part of that. Instead, we're going to spend all of our training on teaching you what I wish someone would have taught me when I was starting out: *How I could help others while getting highly paid for sharing my message, story and how-to advice. In essence, you're going to learn how to become a Big Money Speaker®!* What's amazing is, people begin loudly applauding every single time because that is exactly what they desire!

So what does this mean for you? It's simple. Please understand there are two sides to every business. One side is your passion, mission and desire to help others. And the second side is called the business, especially marketing. Most people fail in business because they don't realize they should be spending the majority of their time focused on marketing.

It's very simple. If people don't know about you and the value you bring to the marketplace, then they can't buy from you. Anybody who doesn't want to believe this truth won't be in business very long.

Marketing is not something you do to people. It's not manipulation. It's something you do for people by letting them know you and your great value exists. So it's ok to market! You're not a bad person if you market, because if what you do does what I call AME (Adds Value, Makes a Difference and Enriches Lives) why wouldn't you want everyone to know about it? Marketing isn't trickery and manipulation. You're simply letting people know that you exist; so tell everybody and remember: You are NOT in the (fill-in-the-blank) business! You are in the business of marketing your business!

LESSON 2:
Remove the Bib and Replace It with a Napkin!

You may remember me from being featured on the hit ABC TV show, "Secret Millionaire." If you do not know of the show, here is the basic premise from show promotions:

> *"What happens when business motivational speaker and self-made millionaire James Malinchak is picked up by an ABC television crew, placed on an airplane with no money, credit cards, cell phone, laptop or watch, and is whisked off to an impoverished neighborhood, where he had to live undercover and survive on $44.66 cents for a week?*
>
> *The show features Malinchak leaving his current lifestyle in search of real-life heroes who are making a difference in their local community. He ultimately reveals himself as a millionaire and rewards them with a portion of his own money to further their cause by gifting them with checks of his own money totaling over $100,000. If you watched ABC's 'Secret Millionaire' you know that James is no ordinary entrepreneur. He is a self-made millionaire with a strong passion for giving back and serving others."*

Amazingly, over 10 MIILLION people watched me on the show! Whether I am speaking at a business conference, consulting for an entrepreneur, walking through an airport or just hanging out at a coffee shop, I always seem to get asked the same question: *"How did living undercover on* Secret Millionaire *and writing checks to help others affect you?"*

My answer is always the same. The greatest gift you can receive is knowing you have made a positive difference in the lives of others. The show reminded me of that gift!

I have been teaching this concept for over 20 years in my speaking presentations by standing on stage and tucking a bib under my chin. I say the following to audiences.

> "This is what most people do when they network, they approach people with an invisible bib placed under their chin. We have been programmed since birth to go through life wearing a bib, which means being a taker by expecting everyone to serve and give to us.

But how you really make a difference in the world is by making the decision to remove that bib from under your chin and placing it over your forearm and approaching everyone with the mindset and spirit of serving them. Asking yourself: How can I serve? What can I do for each person I meet? That's how you make a real difference and that is how you can rapidly attract people to want to associate and do business with you!"

I have a friend who is an NBA coach who says that he puts in a full year of serving before he ever asks a person for anything. He did it to me, and I didn't even realize it! The guy just kept serving, serving, serving, giving, giving, giving. A year and a half later he decided to start a speaking business, and who was the first person he called for coaching and help? Me! At that point I didn't even think about charging him my usual high five-figure consulting fee because of how much he served and poured into my life the previous twelve months.

My Big Money Speaker® training has been called "The World's #1 Speaker Training" for years. I've been blessed to teach people from over 40 countries how to become Big Money Speakers® sharing their message, story and how-to advice.

I took the letters BMS and turned it into an acronym that is easy to remember that will allow you to get in with anyone, anytime and anyplace by always serving (wearing a napkin), never taking (wearing a bib).

B stands for **Buyer**, meaning whomever you are trying to get in with, think like that person and determine what it is they want.

M stands for **Match**, meaning after you determine what it is they want, ask yourself how you can match what they want (aka, help them get it).

S stands for **Solve**, meaning make sure you're helping to solve their challenge when matching what the buyer wants.

I'll give you a real-life example. Kevin Harrington, one of the original sharks on the hit business TV show, *Shark Tank*, is a man responsible for generating five billion dollars in sales. We met for the first time at an event in San Diego, even though he really didn't know who I was. I was standing in the back of the convention meeting room listening to him being interviewed on stage, while having my BMS antennae up focusing on trying to serve him (aka, wearing a napkin, not a bib).

The interviewer said, *"Kevin, you've been traveling all over the place to speak at events."*

Kevin kind of rolled his eyes and said, *"Yah, I love speaking,* meeting and helping people, but the traveling starts to tire you out."

Immediately, I knew exactly what I needed to do to serve Kevin. After finishing the interview and exiting the stage, at least 200 people rushed him and started pitching him saying things like: "Could you invest in my company? Could you put me on TV?" In essence, they were all about themselves in their approach by choosing to wear bibs (being takers), rather than wearing napkins (being servers).

The key was to approach him with the focus on BMS (Buyer, Match, Solve). After all others finished talking with him, I approached Kevin with the BMS formula and the mental image of a napkin over my forearm with the intention of being a server.

I said, *"Excuse me Kevin. You don't know me, but my name is James Malinchak."*

Kevin said, *"Hi, James. Nice meeting you."*

I then said, *"Kevin, I can help to solve your problem for you."*

He said, *"What?"*

I repeated, *"Kevin, I can help to solve your problem for you."*

He looked at me strangely while asking, *"What's my problem?"*

I then said, *"You live in South Florida, right? Why are you flying all over the place in order to speak? Why don't you just speak for all the conventions coming to Tampa, Orlando and Miami so you can do what you love which is speaking, yet you can be at home in your bed every night and eliminate tiring yourself out by flying all over the place?"*

He said, *"Oh my gosh, I would love that. I just don't know how to do it."*

I then said, *"That's why I moved to Las Vegas 17 years ago. I love speaking but got tired of traveling all over the place. When I realized there are over 20,000 conventions that come to Las Vegas each year, I decided to move there and market to all of the Vegas conventions so I could eliminate traveling and be at home while doing what I love—speaking and helping others."*

"I could get on the phone with you for less than 30 minutes and teach you how to get directly to all the event coordinators bringing their conventions to Tampa, Orlando and Miami so you can do the same as I did for Las Vegas.

Would that be of service to you? Would that solve your problem?"

He was so excited about connecting with me that he immediately called me so that I could teach him my strategy (aka, serve him). Kevin was so grateful that I helped solve his problem that he actually said the following in a video interview: *"The first time I met James, he gave me an idea that has been a multi-million-dollar idea for me personally!"*

Since that initial "serving" call a few years ago, Kevin and I have become dear friends and have worked together on many projects and continue to do so.

So what does this mean for you? It's simple. If you really want to make a difference in the lives of others and rapidly attract people to want to associate and do business with you, then always ask yourself: *How can I serve? What can I do for each person I meet? In essence, always lead with a napkin, never a bib.*

LESSON 3:
The Top Achiever Triangle:
Mindset, Skillset and Getting Off Your Assets!

I believe there are three foundational qualities that make top achievers successful. The first is mindset. Not wishful, pie-in-the-sky, just think happy thoughts-type of thinking! I mean actually changing your mindset and reprogramming yourself consistently on a daily, weekly, monthly and yearly basis to think on higher levels.

But that is only the first piece of the top achiever triangle. Having the right mindset alone will not get you higher levels of success. Much is taught on the subjects of mindset and breaking through limiting beliefs. But mindset alone is incomplete in the top achiever triangle.

The second part of the top achiever triangle needed is skillset. You actually must learn and acquire certain skills. These are specific, tangible, real-world tactics and techniques that are required for the success in any endeavor. Meaning WHAT will you do daily as far as action-taking strategies?

Mindset and skillset are essential, but with only them you will not experience top achiever success levels. The third part of the top achiever triangle needed is, you must get off your assets! Meaning, HOW will you get yourself to take action? People often make excuses and blame their lack of success on various factors, rather than taking responsibility for their own lack of action. The truth is, the universe rewards speed and implementation.

ONE LAST MESSAGE FOR YOU...

My mission with my teachings is always the same: to serve you and made a positive difference in your life by inspiring you to think and act differently. My hope is that you have become more inspired and empowered to BE MORE, DO MORE and ACHIEVE MORE!

Whether you achieve your dreams and goals is solely up to you. No one can promise or guarantee what level of success you will achieve. However, by following simple success strategies like those in this book, YOU CAN begin to accomplish anything you desire.

YOU CAN DO IT–THE TIME TO START IS NOW!

TWEETABLE
You Are NOT in the (fill-in-the-blank) Business! You Are in the Business of Marketing Your Business!

James Malinchak is recognized as one of the most requested, in-demand business and motivational keynote speakers and marketing consultants in the world, and speaks for groups ranging from 20-20,000+.

*James was **featured on the Hit ABC TV Show, Secret Millionaire**, has authored 20 books, delivered 1,000+ consultations and has delivered over 3,000+ presentations for corporations, associations, business groups, colleges, universities and youth organizations worldwide.*

*James is the **behind-the-scenes, go-to Speaker Marketing Advisor** for many top celebrities, top authors, speakers, thought-leaders, professional athletes & sports coaches. James Big Money Speaker® training is legendary and has become known as "The World's #1 Speaker Training" for anyone wanting to get highly paid sharing their mission, message, story and how-to advice!*

*Because you are reading this, you are entitled to receive a FREE Copy of James' Best-Selling Book, Millionaire Success Secrets. **Receive Your FREE Hard-Cover Book (a FREE $25 value) Plus 3 FREE Bonus Training Videos (a FREE $997 value) by visiting: www.MillionaireFreeBook.com***

WHAT OTHERS ARE SAYING

"Kyle, Friendship is wealth and you make me a rich man. Thanks for being a friend and partner all these years. Love and Respect!"

— **Jim Rohn (1930-2009), America's Foremost Business Philsopher**

"Kyle is simply a marketing genius! Every marketing dilemma I have ever had, Kyle has given me the brilliant and elegant solution on the spot. His consulting has saved and earned me hundreds of thousands of dollars over the years."

— **Darren Hardy, Former Publisher *SUCCESS* magazine**

"I have worked closely with Kyle Wilson for 25 years. He is one of the best all-around marketers, promoters, business-builders and entrepreneurs in the business today. We have generated more than a million dollars together."

— **Brian Tracy, Author of *The Psychology of Achievement***

"Kyle Wilson, single handedly changed the way I look at life! And the way I participate in my own! His wisdom, loyalty and commitment to seeing people soar is unmatched in the industry. He is a spring board, sounding board and ultimately, a launch pad for anyone committed to pursuing their deepest dreams and ultimate goals! He is the most authentic mentor, friend and business parter I've ever had."

— **Erika De La Cruz, TV & Media Host, Speaker, Trainer and Author of *Passionistas***

"Kyle is one of my old and dear friends and one of the smartest marketing guys I have had the opportunity to work with. He is the scrappy marketing guy. What I mean by that is, there are lots of guys who will put out business plans and do all kinds of nonsense and swing for home runs. Kyle is the real deal and finds ways to create product, add value, help people, build community, he's unbelievable."

— **Eric Worre, Founder of Network Marketing Pro and International Best-Selling Author of *Go Pro – 7 Steps to Becoming a Network Marketing Professional***

"If wanting to break into the speaker, author, marketing world, no one knows and does it better than my 10 year friend, Kyle Wilson. He is responsible for millions of people having access to the brilliant wisdom of Jim Rohn and so many other business thought leaders. He attracts the best people to his Inner Circle, something I'm proud to be a part of. I'm also excited to be working on a new book with Kyle, Lessons From Sports. *Honored by his friendship."*

— **Newy Scruggs, 7x Emmy-Winning Broadcaster**

190

"Kyle is a valued friend, a marketing superstar and one of the most knowledgeable people in the personal development industry."
— **Robin Sharma, Best-Selling Author of *The Monk Who Sold His Ferrari***

"Kyle Wilson is not only one of my most valued friends and mentors, he is a marketing genius and brilliant business man always providing the most honest and insightful solutions to any challenge. I am honored to have him as my book partner and life long counterpart."
— **Jeanette Ortega, Best-Selling Author of *The Little Black Book of Fitness* & Celebrity Fitness Trainer**

"Kyle is one of the wisest and most brilliant marketing consultants in the world. He is the man behind the great marketing of Jim Rohn and so many other personal development legends. He is not only someone I've enjoyed collaborating and working with for over two decades, but also a close and valued friend. I recommend Kyle without equivocation."
— **Mark Victor Hansen, Co-Creator of *Chicken Soup for the Soul***

"Kyle Wilson is the best marketer I know. In the 20 years I have known him, everything he touches and every idea he generates turns into money. If you're looking for a degree of fame and a higher degree of wealth, I recommend you connect with Kyle as fast as you can."
— **Jeffrey Gitomer, Author of *The Little Red Book of Selling***

"Over the last 25 years, we've done several things together. Kyle is the only guy who has always under-promised and over-delivered on anything we have done together."
— **Tom Ziglar, CEO of Ziglar, Inc.**

"Kyle Wilson's insight, marketing acumen and business knowledge are guru level. His consulting, friendship and brilliant solutions have changed the trajectory of my career and life. His strategies don't just elevate, they transform you and your brand. "
— **Olenka Cullinan, Speaker, Passionista, Founder of Rising Tycoons & #iStartFirst Bossbabe Bootcamps**

GET CONNECTED

To Learn More About the
Kyle Wilson Inner Circle Mastermind

Go To KyleWilsonMastermind.com
or send an email to info@kylewilson.com
with *Inner Circle* in the Subject.

For details on upcoming events

Go to KyleWilsonEvents.com

Receive Your Special Bonuses for Buying
the *Life-Defining Moments* Book

Send an Email to
info@LessonsFromDefiningMoments.com
with *Gifts* in the subject